T0116975

REFLECTIONS OF A SERIAL ENTREPRENEUR

BUD STODDARD

iUniverse, Inc.
New York Bloomington

Reflections of a Serial Entrepreneur

Copyright © 2010 Bud Stoddard

iUniverse books may be ordered through booksellers or by contacting:

iUniverse
1663 Liberty Drive
Bloomington, IN 47403
www.iuniverse.com
1-800-Authors (1-800-288-4677)

ISBN: 978-1-4502-0238-1 (pbk)
ISBN: 978-1-4502-0240-4 (cloth)
ISBN: 978-1-4502-0239-8 (ebook)

Printed in the United States of America

iUniverse rev. date: 1/19/10

INTRODUCTION

Why take advice from a guy named Bud?

I am about to tell you almost everything you need to know about starting your company. So before we go there I need to convince you that I know what I am talking about and am a credible source. Allow me to give you a brief resume of my entrepreneurial activities over the past thirty years to try to convince you that I am well equipped to write on this subject.

It started in college, where I had a steam bath in my fraternity house and charged my brothers a small fee to use it. It clearly was not a big financial success, but I got my feet wet (no pun here) in starting companies. Following a stint in the U.S. Army, I joined my entrepreneur dad and went into the business of selling and servicing calculators and copiers to business. I spent several years there and was exposed to all the challenges of being involved in a small company of twenty-five employees. Although it was fun, challenging, and very educational, it was not my creation and I resigned two weeks after my thirtieth birthday to go off and start my very first company.

I started a company called MicroMedia of New England that filmed business documents for businesses. We had many Kodak cameras and hired moms on a part-time basis to prepare and film documents on microfilm and microfiche in Needham, Massachusetts. During the 1980s the first edition of bank consolidation occurred, and, as some of the region's banks bought their smaller rivals, we carted thousand of boxes of records to our facility and delivered boxes of microfilm back to the client. Thousands of boxes were miniaturized and indexed to make them instantly retrievable. We always prepared at least two copies of film or fiche for the customer, one to use in the business and one to store safely in the archive. After suggesting to the client they store the archive copy of the film at Iron Mountain, it was time to birth company number 2. I sold the company in the mid-'80s and the successor company is still thriving today as the same business, named SourceCorp.

Next was DataVault Corporation, a company dedicated to storing vital corporate records in a highly secure facility to include an underground Nike missile site in southeastern Massachusetts. It came from customer demand, the best reason to start a company, as companies that had great confidence in MicroMedia asked us to be the custodians of their film, fiche, tapes, and, later, documents. I sold this company to Iron Mountain in 1996 and joined the company as a vice president of sales for two years.

When the Internet was in its early years and PCs were starting to propagate, we launched TeleVault Technology, a company that backed up the customer's data over telephone lines and Internet connections and sent that data to our highly secure data center. *This company failed*, but we learned two very important lessons. One, pay your taxes. Our software supplier was literally shut down by the state of California for failure to pay payroll taxes. Two, timing is everything in business. If a great idea is too early for the market (we were), it will be difficult to succeed.

I took a hiatus in the late '90s, deciding to join Iron Mountain and trying my hand at "corporate America" for two years. As I had a boss and bureaucracy at the company, I decided it was time to become an entrepreneur for a fourth time. This was challenging, as I had a very strict noncompete agreement which I signed when I sold DataVault to Iron Mountain. I got very creative and convinced the CEO to let me out of my noncompete in exchange for 10 percent ownership in the company.

I launched Recovery Solutions, online data backup over the Internet, the very same business as TeleVault, but six years later. We subsequently changed our name to AmeriVault, and the company became a de facto leader in an emerging industry. We sold the company last year.

Finally, so far at least, I started Certified Backup, an economy version of AmeriVault. AmeriVault was a premium brand, and we didn't want to discount or taint our brand, so we started Certified Backup to bring an economy solution to very small business. This was a very effective strategy. The company was later acquired by AmeriVault.

In the past twenty-five-plus years I have started five companies, recruited and hired over three hundred employees, and acquired thousands of customers.

I certainly don't have all the answers or, for that matter, all of the questions or challenges, But I am highly confident that I have packed this book with a great deal of critical information that will better equip you for success. So dig in and enjoy.

— Chapter One —

Want It

Starting a business is no doubt one of the most demanding challenges that you will undertake in your life. It's hard work! More important than the idea, the timing, the business model, or the financing, is your attitude. You have to want it badly and be willing to make many sacrifices. There will be endless hurdles, many disappointments, and lots of nos from potential customers. The only thing that will keep you going during these times is a persistence and perseverance second to none.

Not everyone is cut out to be an entrepreneur, so perhaps before you take the plunge and hit up Uncle Hymie for some start-up capital, you need to do a self-assessment and make sure you have what it takes.

This entrepreneur favors the idea that entrepreneurs are born and not made. This is a debate that we will not address here. Some, but certainly not all, of the things you will need are the following:

- An ability to sell to a perfect stranger
- Some financial acumen
- A very good idea
- The ability to execute your plan
- People skills

- Good communication, both verbal and written
- An ability to attract the top people
- A means to differentiate from all others
- The will to win
- A no-quit attitude
- A commitment to success and the perseverance to get there

Being repeatedly late for dinner, missing a baseball game or dance recital, being late for a family gathering, and constantly apologizing to your spouse for being late or absent are a given. If you're not willing to disappoint family and friends, you probably won't make it.

Not on the above list but terribly important to success is a supportive spouse. I can honestly say that I would not have been triumphant in starting five successful companies had I not been married to a woman who had tremendous faith in me and would tolerate my apologies for one more missed soccer game. And don't make the mistake of *assuming your spouse will support you.* The wedding vows we took say for better or for worse and for richer or for poorer, but they don't say anything about starting a company.

You will likely come close to failure on numerous occasions on your way to success. Having the stomach to experience that and the guts to fight your way through it are the ticket to admission. This will not be easy, but it will be worth it. Therefore, before you write that business plan, take an inventory and make sure *you really want it.*

— CHAPTER TWO —

DO I NEED A BUSINESS PLAN?

The answer is, emphatically, *yes*. The next question becomes: what does my business plan include and how long should it be?

A phenomenon of the dot-com era was robust and lengthy business plans that often spanned forty pages or more and included excruciating details for angels and venture capitalists to sink their teeth into. In reality, much of what was in those plans never got read in detail. At best it got scanned by junior associates, as the more senior people had no time to read or interest in reading an overly laborious business plan. Many software programs were developed to write plans, and Excel spreadsheets included reams of financial data that often projected out five years or more. There was too much detail as to expenses, as well as grandiose revenue projections that often resembled a hockey stick in terms of their sales growth and velocity. Lackluster ideas, like buying groceries, drugs, and toys on the Internet, were embellished by long business plans. A herd mentality resulted in funding those plans, only to cost all of the investors all of their money in subsequent times. Some months after the grocery shopping on the Net idea crashed and burned, my wife told me that she knew that would never work. I questioned her as to why. She told me she not only went to the supermarket to buy groceries but to see friends and neighbors and to chat. She couldn't chat (at least at that point in time) on the Web. Incidentally, she just established a Facebook account.

So, if the fifty-page business plan with reams of financial projections is not the answer, what should your plan include?

The first point I want to make is, who is the plan written for? Who is the audience? Number one, it is for you, the entrepreneur. It forces you to get your ideas on paper and sharpen your focus. Getting the business condensed into writing will help you focus on the business and what you are trying to accomplish.

The second audience group is the potential investors, whether they are friends, family, angels, or institutional venture investors. You need a sharp, meaningful plan to convince these people you have a good idea and a large market, and you are the right person to capitalize on that opportunity.

I would suggest a business plan of eight to fourteen pages. That is plenty if you choose your content carefully. There are a number of questions to focus on:

- What problem are you trying to solve? Is there a need in the marketplace?
- How big a market is it?
- What is your product, service, or technology and how will that solve the problem?
- Who are the founders and what qualifies them to execute on the plan?
- How much capital do you need, what are you going to do with the money, and how will the investors be paid back?
- Is there something unique and patentable in your plan? If you are a technology company, can you protect with patents on the software, the process, or the business model?
- What is the go-to market strategy? This is a big one and should include all manner of distribution and customer acquisition.

- What are the barriers to entry? How difficult is it for others to enter your market and compete with you?
- Who is the competition, and what do you know about them? Is there a market leader at present?
- What are the inherent risks?
- Can you provide a three-year financial summary?

That's it, no more, no less. A page on each subject that answers the question is more than sufficient. If it is well thought out and well written, this is all you need. The plan will really help you, as the entrepreneur, to focus and answer the hard questions. It will also provide a template when you are ready to approach investors for funding. Develop a written plan and also a PowerPoint presentation, and rehearse your pitch until you can wake up in the middle of the night and nail it with no preparation.

An additional point needs to be made. It seems obvious that we should all have an "elevator pitch" and that it's easy. It is not. Have a concise (fifteen seconds and three sentences at most) pitch that will answer the question *what business are you in*?

I am continually amazed at the number of established or aspiring entrepreneurs that cannot *answer that question*. I have heard scores of entrepreneurs ramble on, and when finished, I still have no idea what they do. I am a reasonably smart guy, who understands business, so I get it. If you cannot give me a fifteen-second explanation that I understand, there is something wrong with your pitch. I know it sounds painfully obvious, but trust me when I tell you that many cannot do it. Start with your "elevator pitch" and nail it. It is harder than you might think.

One final point: Get excited. Passion, commitment, undying enthusiasm, however you define it is, without a doubt the most important trait of a successful entrepreneur. If you are not excited about your launch, how can you expect others to be? Enthusiasm is contagious.

— CHAPTER THREE —

NO BEST TIME TO START

It would be very easy, in light of the current economic downturn, to postpone launching your business until the economy improves. In fact, far more people will *not do it* this year than will. It takes courage to launch at this time, but I say go for it. If you have a compelling business idea and the passion to execute it, there is no better time than the present. In fact, for many reasons, starting in a downturn provides some advantages. For starters, you may:

- Attract top people more easily than in robust times.
- Secure office or production space at a good price.
- Get good deals on services like marketing, because firms are eager for new business.
- Get funds at very low interest rates. Yes, banks are lending.
- Be able to barter for services.
- Get special billing terms.
- Grow share while others have gone defensive and pulled in their horns.

If your current employer is looking at downsizing, by raising your hand and volunteering, you may get a big enough package to fund your start-up. It is very easy to find a reason to delay, but it takes enormous courage to make the leap in uncertain economic times, which we are in now.

In these economic times I might do a little more market research to test my idea before taking the plunge. A simple and cost-effective way to do that research is by talking to potential customers of your service. This can be done by phone or in person, but I would prefer to do these interviews in person. There are three things I want to find out from the prospect during an interview. First, does the customer have a need for the product or service that I sell? Two, does the prospect expect to buy that product or service in the next few months? And three, would the prospect consider buying that service from a new company— yours?

A word to the wise is appropriate here. Many companies will not buy from a brand-new company. They just do not want the risk that you may fail, and you can probably not change their minds. Some companies are more open to doing business with a newer company, but you must convince them you are secure and will be around for a long time. If you are successful in doing that, you may have a chance to get the order. You must give them some special reason for doing business with you, such as a special price, extra service, free goods, a money-back guarantee, twenty-four-hour service or something different from what they can get from all of your competitors. (See more about being different in the chapter Differentiate or Die). If you offer a similar product or service at a similar price with similar service, you will lose; you will not get the order.

One more caveat. Many sales people think they are special, and their customers buy from them, not their company. They feel they have the customer's loyalty and would get their business even if they were on their own or went to work for a competitor. Do not overestimate you customer loyalty. When you go out and start your business and come back to those very same clients you will, no doubt, sense some reservations on their part. You have no track record, no customers, and no sales. You have been in business for a month and expect the client to give you their business. Do not make this naïve assumption, as I assure you that you will be disappointed.

A great idea is a great idea, regardless of the state of the economy. If you are ready, if you have the capital, if you have written the business plan, if your spouse is on board, and if you want this venture more than anything else, then go for it, The time still is right.

— Chapter Four —

Good Ideas Prevail

A good idea with great execution is better than a great idea with poor or adequate execution. Many large companies have done this successfully for years. In fact, it is a known fact that most unique innovation doesn't come from large, established companies but rather from small entrepreneurial start-ups (Apple may be the exception to this rule).

For years, large companies have sold unspectacular goods and services against competitors with far superior goods and services. There are a number of reasons for this ostensible phenomenon. Large companies don't innovate; prospects don't take risk in buying from the safe supplier; and the smaller, innovative company doesn't normally have the funds, marketing sales channels, and PR to get noticed against the bigger and less-spectacular rival.

But this commitment to mediocrity and to products and services that are "just good enough" makes these same market leaders vulnerable. If you have a superior, differentiated service, you can win the business and steal the business from the eight-hundred-pound gorilla. *And you must differentiate.* If you do the same thing they do, in the same way, with similar service, and a similar price, the established players will kick your butt.

Let me share a brief story about commitment to mediocrity at the large company. A decade ago I was working for a Fortune

500 company. I was there as vice president of strategic sales. This was a new experience for me, working in corporate America. The last time I had done this was my first job after graduating from college, at Proctor & Gamble. I was committed to the company, highly motivated, and doing my best to excel in my new environment.

Several sales and marketing types were in a conference room discussing customer service as well as penetrating and servicing larger accounts. During the conversation, the VP of marketing declared in no uncertain terms that we could not provide great service, as it *cost too much money*. I laughed out loud and seriously thought he was making a joke. Because I was the new guy, everyone else in the room knew he did not make jokes and was completely serious. It was a bit embarrassing, but I survived the moment. It was a learning lesson, but I then realized he was serious and the company was committed to delivering "just good enough" service. Mediocrity was not only acceptable but was a *goal*. Be "just good enough" and the customer won't go away.

Shortly after this defining meeting, I made the decision to leave the company and start a fifth company, one that would deliver killer customer service. The customer deserved it, and I would figure a way to do it cost effectively.

Not everyone who starts his or her own business has a great idea. That may not stop them, and it shouldn't, from launching, as they probably think they do have a great idea. In the last several months, in my new role as angel investor and a board member, I have read many business plans from companies looking for funding. I have been amazed at many of the plans and ideas they promote. The Web has changed everything, and many businesses are just Web sites. That is okay. Many of these plans don't have a sound, defensible business, won't make it in the marketplace, and probably shouldn't get funding. Many will. We are the land of entrepreneurship, and if the founder is committed and excited and can convince others of his/her passion, then that person deserves a shot.

I want to urge you to do due diligence on your idea and plan. Vet it carefully and fully. Talk to prospects, potential customers, suppliers and investors, and ask them if they would be willing to pay money for your product or service, and, if so, how much? Market research is easy and inexpensive and just may save you the embarrassment of losing the money that Uncle Hymie invested in your great business idea that nobody was willing to buy.

A good idea with great execution will prevail over a great idea with poor execution, but a dumb idea will just lose all your investors' money. Losing your investors' money is not a good outcome.

— Chapter Five —

Don't Start a Company Because You Are Unemployed

It is no accident that I chose this time to write a book. One of the primary drivers for me was the state of the economy and the climbing unemployment rolls across the country. I have a few thoughts on this subject.

First, there is always the question of when is a good time to start a business. Should I start a company in good times or bad? When the economy is in a funk, should I wait until it improves before I take the plunge?

As I look back on my entrepreneurial history, although I didn't know it at the time, I started four companies when the country was in an economic decline. I was probably too naïve at the time to understand macroeconomics and know things weren't very good. I started companies in 1978, 1982, 1998 and 2002. I borrowed money when the prime was 18 percent (this is not a typo) in order to buy the commercial building my first company was located in and bought an underground missile site in 1990 with the help of an SBA loan. Fortunately, in spite of my youthful naïveté and ignorance to where the Dow was, all companies were successful, and I sold three of the four at a significant profit, including my last company in mid-2008 just as the markets crashed again.

What is my point? The best time to start a company is when *you* are compelled to do so. There are certainly advantages to starting when things are good, and, yes, there are advantages when things are bad. It is rather obvious as to the many advantages of starting a business in robust economic times. Thus, I will forego reciting those advantages and talk about starting in bad times.

This is anti-intuitive. Most would-be entrepreneurs will forego the decision, perhaps out of fear or the urging of friends and family, and all advice will be, why don't you wait until things get better and the economy improves? Here are some of the key reasons to start in the downturn.

Most will defer. Most will not start now. So reason one is exactly that; you will have less competition for everything: capital, employees, space, vendors and suppliers, ideas, resources of all types.

A great idea is a great idea regardless of the economic condition of the country. If you are motivated to launch and you are 100 percent committed, then go for it now.

Although some might argue that capital is scarce and VCs and angels are very conservative now and reserving most capital for their current portfolio companies, they still have dry powder to put to work. They are seeing fewer business plans, so there is a lot less competition for that capital. They might also strike deals more advantageous to the entrepreneur if they are seeing fewer deals. Angels may opt for start-ups, for if they put capital in the stock market in the last year they definitely have a negative return thus far.

Top-notch employees are easier to recruit and more affordable than in robust times. Also, if individuals feel their job may be at risk as their company has had recent layoffs, they are far more likely to look favorably at a start-up. And the big salaries and fat option packages prevalent in 1999-2001 are not necessary to recruit star talent.

Vendors and suppliers are hungry for business and will cut you more favorable deals to get your business in these trying times.

Barter gains in popularity during down times. You may be able to barter your services for other services that those companies offer and you need.

Customers are desperate to cut costs, and if your product or service will save them money versus their current supplier, they will be less loyal and more likely to do business with the company that can save them money.

Your established competitors may have downsized recently. If they are reducing staff and reducing expenses, they are probably not paying as much attention to their installed base of clients, and so it is a good time to strike and lure their customers away.

The Internet has provided so many options that make it easier and far less costly to launch a new company, so you may need less start capital than you needed in previous years (See my chapter on sales and lead gen.)

So, if you have the right idea, the passion to succeed, and relentless commitment to success, *go for it now*. There is no better time than the present.

Now, that I have encouraged you to move forward without delay despite the down economy, I have one large caveat: *Do not start your own company because you are unemployed, and you need a job. You start a company to create a great company, not to create a job for yourself.*

When unemployment rates go up, there is a greater tendency for people to launch their own businesses. Those people figure, "I was good at my job; I have a marketable skill, and people will pay for my services. This is definitely a bad idea, and the wrong motivation to start your own business. Becoming an independent consultant because you are unemployed is the wrong motivation. And you will likely bail if someone offers you a job. So many individuals think it is easy to do this, but you need customers as well as a marketable skill. It is a far different world out there when you have to go out and sell your services and convince prospects they should pay you a premium price for those services. And lastly, newly minted entrepreneurs often work for free or below market salaries to get started. I worked for free for eighteen months (absolutely no salary; try selling that idea to your spouse) when I launched AmeriVault, but, fortunately, I was in a financial position where I could do that. Most people are not in that position when they launch their first company.

If you see starting a company as an easy or convenient way to secure employment, please heed my advice, and you will save yourself a lot of disappointment, time, money, and frustration.

Start a company for all the right reasons, and creating a job for yourself is seldom, if ever, the right reason.

— CHAPTER SIX —

THE NAME GAME

Picking a company name is an important and emotional decision. It will be with you forever.

There are at least two schools of thought relative to selecting a name. The first, and the one that I favor, would be to select a name that says what you do.

Examples of this method would be DataVault, SalesForce. com, Ford Motor Company, and BankAmerica. The name indicates what you do and doesn't keep the prospect guessing. It suggests to the prospect or customer that you store data, build sales management software, build and sell automobiles, or are a bank and make loans.

The other school of thought is to select one of those fancy made-up names that a marketing consultant comes up with. Examples of this are Altria, Venyu, Rezziliant, Cognizant, and Google.

There are marketing and naming companies that charge millions of dollars, yes, millions, to come up with names for companies. It is a big business but probably not an option for you as a start-up entrepreneur. Be creative. Ask friends, neighbors, and relatives for their help. Establish a short list of company names as you go, and something will come to you that you are excited about without spending millions. And if you are one of those people without a creative bone in your body, there is also a fairly new trend that is quite simple. Take a word you know and spell it backwards. I am not kidding. Examples of this method are SEPATON (NO TAPES spelled backwards) and XOBNI (IN BOX spelled backwards).

However, the real issue is to secure a name for which you can secure the domain name. So XXcompany.com is what you need to have, not dot net or dot org or any other dot anything. *Dot com only.*

The challenge is that every three- and four-letter combination in the English language followed by dot com is already registered with a domain registration company. Yes, that is correct and hard to believe, but every three- or four-letter combination in the English language is already registered with a domain registry. The likelihood of getting a company name followed by dot com, or that is not already trademark registered or used by another company in your industry, is remote.

But it can be done. Many of the dot com names that are registered are not in use and may be purchased from the owner. It is easy to find and purchase these names if you really want the name and are willing to pay for it.

One of the reasons I favor the real name, not the made-up name, is because of the dominant use of search engines in marketing today. If I know the name AmeriVault and want to key it into a search engine, I will probably spell it correctly and land at the correct site. If I try to key in the name VenYU, I will more than likely spell it VENUE and not find the right site. The likelihood of keying VenYU is remote. In this day and age, search engines are vital to your success. You must make sure your company name is easy to spell and search engine friendly. The Internet, specifically search engines, is the way we find things today. Google is fast becoming a verb, much to Microsoft's dismay, and we will increasingly find products, services, people, and companies with search engines like Google, Bing, and Yahoo.

Some companies have created names with letters in them such as AAMaintenance or ABC Waste Disposal. This was most likely done for positioning in the phone book or yellow pages. Well, the yellow pages have become a dinosaur and been replaced by the Internet and search engines, so do not name your company this way. It is also, in my opinion, small sounding, and we want a company name that is big, powerful, national, even global in nature. Think big, not small, when naming your company.

One final word, resist the urge to name the company after yourself. It is a shallow idea and doesn't provide any clue as to what you do. Put your ego in the closet and chose a big-sounding name so that when you go global you don't have to change it. Whether you chose the traditional naming convention or the made-up name convention, either is far superior to naming the company after yourself.

— CHAPTER SEVEN —

INTEGRITY

You cannot be honest most of the time.

Recently a Massachusetts politician was caught red-handed, on video no less, stuffing cash into her undergarments. It was a payoff for assisting a citizen in obtaining a license of some sort in Boston, Massachusetts. When a supporter was asked by a local television reporter what he thought of this incident, he commented: "many other public officials have accepted bribes far larger than $25,000." I was incredulous when I saw the report. Obviously, this individual believed the payoff was "okay" because others had stolen more.

One is either honest or dishonest; you cannot be a little of both. I have accomplished much in my entrepreneurial career, starting five companies and employing hundreds of employees and representing thousands of customers. If there is a single thing I am most proud of, it's the fact that I have never had an employee, customer, stockholder, or supplier come after us for doing the wrong thing or treating someone without integrity—not a single legal complaint or lawsuit in over twenty-five years.

As we all know, if we tell different things to different people, we will eventually get caught in a lie. If we are always truthful, have impeccable integrity, and do the right thing, there will be no worry about getting entangled in a web of lies.

I always encouraged the new and junior staff, once they had been with the company for a period of time and had been adequately trained, to make a decision and do what they think is right relative to their customer. Don't delay or say, "It's not my job." Rather, take a chance and do what is right for the client. In telling the truth, doing the right thing, believing the customer is always right, you will never get into trouble for making the decision. If you believe it may not be the optimum decision, perhaps your manager can review it with you and discuss how you might have made a better decision. Make it a learning experience for the next time the situation arises.

If I found out that you blatantly lied or screwed the customer, I will terminate you on the spot. There is no gray line, it is black and white. Either you are honest or you are not. In my companies, you are *always* honest and deal with 100 percent integrity, period.

Unfortunately, there is a belief among some in our country that businesspeople are all dishonest. If you are successful in business, and especially if you have accumulated some wealth in the process, you must have screwed people or at least taken advantage of someone. The really successful people in business are presumed dishonest and the ones that are not successful are likely the honest ones. Honesty and integrity do not go hand in hand with success in business. I am here to absolutely dispel that inaccuracy. It is the furthest thing from the truth. Sure, there are dishonest people in business, but the vast majority of people in business are honest and treat their customers, employees, suppliers, and shareholders with the highest degree of integrity.

I demanded honesty and integrity in all of my companies, and I urge you to do the same. There is only one way to run a company, and that is the right way. You will be tempted along the way to step over the line. Sometimes it is more difficult to do the right thing and treat people right, but in the end integrity is its own reward.

— Chapter Eight —

Get Out of the House

Better than 50 percent of entrepreneurs start their business part time and work out of the house. Although this is popular, I don't like or recommend that strategy, especially if you keep your day job. It's like watching a video to learn how to ski instead of going to the mountain or how to hit golf balls rather than going to the range. If you are absolutely committed to starting a company, remove the safety net and go for it. It's too easy to fold your tent and give up your dream if you are not 100 percent committed.

When I started my first company, I quit my job, rented some industrial space, signed a lease, and "went for it." I had two young children, ages three and six, and a wife who was a stay-at-home mom (our choice). Failure was not an option, and, knowing that, I was driven to success. I came very close to running out of money, and my one angel investor had cut me off, so the pressure was on. Things worked out well, but I was on the edge. Fear is a great motivator.

As I have said elsewhere, starting a company, for most of us, is one of the largest and most serious decisions you will make in life. Therefore, it is incredibly important that you prepare fully and do the appropriate due diligence before taking the plunge. Think it through thoroughly, write the business plan, and make sure you have adequate capital. Do the market research, interview industry experts, and, most importantly, talk with prospective customers. Take a personal inventory (see chapter one, "Want It.") to determine if you have the right traits to enhance your likelihood of success. After completing all of this preliminary work, if your commitment and passion remains unabated, you are probably ready. Then, and only then, take the plunge, get out of the house, and sign that lease.

As I will reiterate numerous times in this book, this is one of the most important decisions of your life. So do the homework and do not rush into it unprepared. Forcing yourself to write a good business plan (I told you how to do that in chapter two, "Do I Need a Business Plan?") is a great exercise that forces you to get your ideas on paper. Speaking with potential customers will test your concept, and meeting with investors will test your idea and your mettle. Angel investors have money because they are smart and usually accomplished entrepreneurs, and they will ask the tough questions. If you can convince your investors to part with their hard-earned money, then you probably have a very good business idea. Do the work, and then when you are 100 percent committed, get the hell out of the house.

This book will help a lot; I guarantee it. It will answer many, if not all of your questions regarding starting your business. Having done it several times, I am confident that I have included a lot of sage advice to help you along on this journey.

Entrepreneurship is a full-time job, often fifty or sixty hours a week or even more some weeks. While keeping your job and starting your company part time works for some, it is not the preferred method. You are also shortchanging your employer if you launch a company while working for them. You're collecting a full-time salary while working part time, as you are thinking and acting like an entrepreneur during the workweek. Taken to the extreme, that behavior could get you fired or reprimanded and would likely be justified by your employer. Your boss will likely be respectful when you tell them you are leaving the company to start your own business. It is the American dream, after all, and most people have thought about doing it, even if they never have the courage to pull the trigger. When you are ready, resign your job with the appropriate notice, and go become an entrepreneur on a full-time basis.

As I have noted elsewhere, the real estate market is soft in many parts of the country. You can negotiate a very favorable lease right now and perhaps not pay rent for up to six months. You can also get a short-term lease, one year, or just month-to-month rent as a result of the softness in commercial real estate. So you can minimize the risk of renting that office or commercial space, but you are in; you committed once you sign that lease. This is no turning back, and your motivation will be very high.

My preference is not to be a part-time entrepreneur. Rather, be committed to your idea and go for it. The fact that there is no safety net may be scary but in the end will contribute to your success.

— Chapter Nine —

Killer Customer Service

Everybody in business swears they have great customer service. This is just not reality. But you must have it. Customers expect a set of minimum requirements, and outstanding customer service is one of those basic requirements.

Here are some random thoughts that I would like to share in regards to great customer service:

Do what you say you are going to do. Now, you may be thinking, "Wow! This guy is a real genius. How could anyone write something that is so obvious in his book? The guy isn't a genius; he's an idiot." We have all had positive and negative customer experiences. Doing what you say you are going to do has an impact on the customer. At my last company we instructed our service engineers to tell the customer what to expect and when. If he or she needed to do some work and then call the customer, the employee must tell them, specifically, when they can expect a fix or a callback. If you say, "I will get back to you tomorrow afternoon," *then do it*. It sounds obvious, but it is amazing how many companies could improve service if they just did this and nothing else. Recently, we were having a new garbage disposal installed at the house. Our plumber, though competent, was not the most reliable person I have dealt with. He left (with the job 90 percent complete) for twenty minutes to get supplies and assured us he would return shortly to finish the job. He didn't return, but he did call later that evening to assure us he would return at 8:00 a.m. the next day. He failed to do this as well. He did ultimately finish the job, but he is now our former plumber. As I write this chapter, I contacted an insurance company regarding a recent tour to Europe that my wife and I had to end early due to a health issue. The very nice woman I talked to ten days earlier had assured me I would get a claims form in two to three days. When I called after ten days had gone by, there was no record and the tracking number I was given ten days earlier was not in the computer. So nice lady number two assured me I would have the form by the end of the day, as I asked her to e-mail it rather than use snail mail. The day ended, and I had not received the form. Needless to say, I am not impressed with this company and will never do business with them again. My mantra is now, "Just do what you say you are going to do." This may sound simple, but many companies fail to get it right.

Technology. Is it a friend or a foe? In our persistent path to lowering costs and improving service, many companies have gone overboard in the use of technology. The one that annoys me the most is the automated attendant (computer voice) which lists so many options (1 for accounts payable, 2 for new accounts, 3 to pay your bill, etc.) that you need to play it again to remember them all. Most of us can remember three or four choices. So don't give us eight before we get to a live person.

Making it impossible to reach *a real person*. My wife was trying to reach the electric company in Florida, as our bill seemed very high. Although she is very Web savvy and used the Internet and telephone to inquire, we could never get to speak with a live person. I got involved and assured her I would find a person for her to speak with. I went on their Web site and found the name of the executive in charge of customer service. When I tried to call her, there was no place on the Web site that listed a phone number. They intentionally had no numbers anywhere, as they did not want customers to call. Rather, they wanted the customer to deal with a problem via the Web or the automated voice. How *arrogant. I did* get through, finally, and let them know how annoyed I was. We did get a very nice customer engineer to come to our house to help us figure out how to lower our bill. But they made the experience painful. Luckily for them, they are a monopoly and therefore can get away with it. Unfortunately for us, we can't fire them!

Push 1 for Spanish and 2 for English. I deal with a very nice community bank in Massachusetts and have for thirty years. They are a well-run organization and provide a great customer experience. I only have one gripe with them. Although I have been a customer forever and cannot speak a word of Spanish, they continually ask whether I want English or Spanish. But Spanish is the first choice. Actually, I flunked Spanish in college and had to switch my major from economics to marketing, as Spanish was required in economics but not for marketing. My bank reminds me every time I call that I suck at Spanish, and it really pisses me off. It is very simple with caller ID for the bank to know it is me calling, and I don't speak Spanish. I would feel the very same way if they asked if I wanted French or Chinese, so I don't want any of my Spanish-speaking readers to be upset with me.

Be very careful about outsourcing customer service. I am a big fan of outsourcing and made a very comfortable living starting and running three companies involved in outsourcing. But I don't believe you should outsource customer service. A big trend in the last decade has been for large companies to outsource customer service to countries in the Far East, where the labor costs are much lower. One of the most notable examples of this trend, and one that was later aborted, was with Dell Computer. They experienced so many customer issues that they later cancelled the contract and brought their service business back to the United States. I have personally been a victim (not with Dell) of the customer service person who I could not understand. It is very frustrating when you have a service issue, and, despite how hard you try, you cannot understand the person on the other end of the phone. Enough said on this subject.

Train your people. More common sense, perhaps, but, again, common sense is not so common. Before you put someone on the phone, give him or her adequate training to answer most of the customer's questions and issues. It will pay dividends. You work so hard to get a customer; do not blow it because your customer service is not up to par.

Always give the customer the option to speak with a real person, if they prefer. Sometimes we are so committed to using technology to try and provide a good experience and lower costs that we forget this. Let the customer have access to people. From time to time we become anxious enough that the only thing that will make us feel better is a real person. Do not deny the customer the feeling of human kindness.

Follow up calls and survey your customers to make sure you are getting it right. Not every call, but perhaps you call 10 percent and survey 40 percent. It is easy and inexpensive, and you will learn a lot. My Jaguar dealer tells me after service that if his rating on service is less that 100 percent, he has failed. I like that, and he washed my car before I left. Now *that's* customer service.

Treat people like you would like to be treated. We have all had the nightmare experience as with our plumber that I described above. We have also all had the excellent service experience. Human nature is that we share the bad experience, but we never tell anybody about the good experience.

Good customer service must be a *given* if you are in business. Do not take this for granted. Work at it every single day you are in business, and get better every day. The customer needs great service and expects it and will not, or *should* not, tolerate anything less.

— CHAPTER TEN —

A SUPPORTIVE SPOUSE

We've all heard the expression "behind every successful man is a great woman," and I am convinced it is absolutely true; a supportive spouse is a critical ingredient to one's success.

But today, that good woman is really a man. The reason is, more women are starting companies today and have done so in the past few years. Studies indicate that for each new company, up to 35 percent are being started by women.

As I have indicated in previous chapters, entrepreneurship is one tough journey. It is no coincidence that over 80 percent of new companies fail within the first five years. There will be enormous challenges during the start-up phase, and in the very early days you are a company of one with no staff or employees. There is no one to fall back on or to share ideas with or to make joint decisions. You are an army of one, and you must make scores of decisions on a daily basis. This is when one really needs the supportive spouse standing behind him or her.

I am one lucky guy, as I have one of the best and most supportive wives that you could ask for. Being a serial entrepreneur, my bride is battle-tested and has been through this process on several occasions. On one occasion, I took a 50 percent pay cut in order to launch, and that was at a time that we had three kids under the age of ten. My wife was working part time, yet we were financially challenged for a couple of years. Later, I took *no salary* for eighteen months. But due to the sale of my former company a couple of years earlier, I was in a stable financial position and was able to do it. However, I did give up a six-figure salary with a Fortune 500 company to take one more run at my passion. Needless to say, I had friends and family members who thought I was absolutely crazy (and perhaps they were right).

Another big family issue when you launch is family health coverage. Family plans often cost about $1,000 per month, and a new company has no health plan. But you need to provide some coverage for the family, which is very expensive. Sitting down with the understanding spouse to share that you are starting a company and we will have no income and no health care coverage for X weeks or months is one tough conversation. But it is a critical one to have. Without that support, things will get worse, and then you are not only putting a company at risk, but your family as well.

Another issue, if the woman is the entrepreneur, is child care. Many couples today share equally in taking care of the kids. Okay, guys, let's be honest about this. In my opinion, we may have a great many talents, but child-rearing doesn't come as easy for us as it does for our wives. Most women do it intuitively, and, in my opinion, it is just not as easy for most of us men. If we are called upon, and we will be, to take a larger role with raising the kids while mom is off building a company, we have a new challenge. Getting three kids out the door and off to school by 7:50 a.m. looks so effortless when they do it, but we all know it really isn't. I'll apologize in advance to the guy readers who feel they are every bit as qualified as their wives to raise the kids, but most of us guys know the real truth. The wives rule.

It's not just about you. This is a family decision. Be sure to take plenty of time and have multiple discussions with your spouse about this major decision. Make sure your spouse is as committed and as passionate about the company as you are.

Your chances of success will grow dramatically if both of you are committed to the dream.

BUD'S BOTTOM LINE TAKEAWAYS

- You have to want it badly and sacrifice
- Attitude and the will to win are paramount
- Write the business plan for *you* first and investors second
- A good idea with great execution wins
- Creating a job for you is not the reason to start a business
- Get out of the house and go for it
- A supportive spouse is a success factor

Chapter Eleven

Calculate the Break Even, Then Double the Money and the Time

Starting a company is hard work. When you do your break-even analysis (how long it will take to get to positive cash flow), double that time and double your needed start-up capital. Entrepreneurs are positive people and tend to see the glass as half full rather than half empty. This is a necessary trait for success. I have personally gone through this break-even analysis exercise a number of times and think I am pretty good at it. Yet I must admit I usually overshoot in my optimism.

In building a business plan and a cash flow analysis, although you attempt to project as accurately as possible, this exercise is really a best-case *guess*. You are projecting (guessing) when customers will buy, how much they will buy, and when they will pay their bills. On the flip side you are projecting expenses like payroll, benefits, rent, utilities, support fees, phone, Internet, insurance, marketing, and a whole host of related costs. The revenue is supposed to grow faster than the expenses, but in real life, often the opposite is true.

Prospects take longer to commit than we expect, unanticipated expenses will arise, and accounts receivable will extend out. The latter is especially true when the economy slows and salespeople overcommit as to *what* they will close and *when*. They don't do this intentionally, but salespeople tend to be optimists, and that is a needed trait for this special breed. Since you are tying your funding to your break-even analysis, you don't want to miss. Running out of cash is a deadly sin and must be avoided at all costs. If you run out of cash and there are no sources of capital available, the end is in sight.

Some ideas to preserve cash are the following:

- You can work with no salary, assuming you can afford to.
- Incent customers to pay early.
- Defer payables as long as possible.
- Get a line of credit in case you need it.
- Three things and *only three* must be paid, no matter *what*:
- First and foremost, pay your employees.
- Pay your phone and Internet.
- Make sure you pay the rent.

Everything else can wait. However, be careful not to keep creditors waiting too long. Word gets out if you pay your bills too slowly, and you may establish the wrong reputation with your creditors.

I have nearly run out of money at least three times in my career, and it is an uncomfortable place to be. When I started my first company, MicroMedia, my investor staked me for a sum of $29,000. I have no idea today how or why we agreed to that amount, not $30,000, not $35,000, not $50,000, but precisely $29,000. I had exhausted the entire amount, and we had a very serious meeting in my offices, and he told me in no uncertain terms that there would be no more money for my fledgling company. It was D-Day for Bud Stoddard and for his new company, MicroMedia. The ultimatum had a positive impact for me and, more importantly, a very good outcome, as I turned the company around, started generating positive cash flow, and never needed an additional dollar of investment. I later sold the company to an investor group and returned a very handsome return to my investor. But we both will always remember that critical day when I almost ran out of cash.

Having lived the above experience, the next time that I did a break-even analysis, for DataVault, I decided to be more conservative and make sure that my plan was cautious and gave me plenty of extra room to make sure that I never ran out of cash again. Despite my best efforts, I was destined to relive the experience of tight cash flow. Revenues didn't come as quickly as we projected, expenses did come as quickly as projected, and once again we were in a tenuous position with our cash needs. A line of credit from a regional bank and later an SBA loan bridged the gap in getting us to a position of positive cash flow.

With company number four, AmeriVault, I raised $5,000,000 in venture capital from an institutional venture capital firm. In 2001 companies were urged to spend that cash on sales and marketing to grow the business quickly. We learned well and invested our cash in several sales offices across the country and were well on our way to world domination in the online backup business. When the dot-com crash crashed hard and quickly, we, like hundreds of others, were short of cash and needed another traunch.

This is when we made the fatal mistake. Although we had all agreed to a two-million-dollar investment, the partners changed their minds the night before the funding and gave us only one million. Coincidentally, that was just enough to give them 51 percent control of the company. Our fatal mistake was naivete.

Right now I would like to share a couple of very important lessons with you, the new entrepreneur, that are very hard to get for most new start-ups. The faster a company grows, the faster you utilize all your cash and create a negative cash flow position. How can I be growing quickly and having success and have no cash. This does not make sense and is hard to comprehend for most of us. Well, it is really not surprising. As I become more successful, I am adding payroll, I am adding inventory, *my* accounts receivable are growing, and my variable expenses are all going up. So, more success means less cash.

Lesson two is that my income statement can look good while my cash-flow statement does not look so good. The P&L tells me how I look on paper and if my gross profit exceeds my expenses. That doesn't mean I have cash to pay all those expenses. Just like the fast growth dilemma, a positive P&L is not the same thing as having plenty of cash.

A final thought on cash and break-even analysis. Have a cushion. If you are raising capital, take 30 to 40 percent *more* than you think you will need. It's much easier to get a little extra in the initial raise than to go back later and try for a second raise. The second round of capital will be more costly to you personally, in terms of equity given up, than it was in the first round. More on this later in chapter 14, on "Venture Capitalists."

Project conservatively and preserve capital at all costs.

— Chapter Twelve —

How to Price

So you are up and running; you're selling services to small to midsized companies, and now you need to do a proposal for pricing and have no idea what to charge or quote. There are numerous options that you could choose:

- Figure out your costs and multiply by two (or three).
- Find out what your competitor charges and undercut him by 10 to 20 percent.
- "Guesstimate" what you should charge.
- Ask your prospect what they are willing to pay.
- Charge based on time and materials.
- Use your gut and put a number on it.

I have always positioned my companies to be in the premium service space. We were high touch, high service, high reliability, available 24/7/365 and high priced. Well, not expensive, but positioned at a premium price above the industry average. This is a very good strategy once you are established, but we need customers to get established.

One needs to be very creative, flexible, and daring to secure those first ten customers. Whether you make money or lose money on those first few clients really doesn't matter. You cannot let your CPA or CFO (if you have one) tell you that you must make 40 to 50 percent gross profit because, again, it does not matter. We are buying credentialed customers who we may use as references.

There are other factors to consider in pricing. Is there an installation cost? Is there paid training? Perhaps you can give one or two months free, or offer deferred or preferred billing. You can even barter part of the cost (see chapter on barter), or maybe the pricing is tiered over time; the options are limitless.

Long term, a strategy is needed. These questions need to be asked: do you want to be the price leader, average price, premium price, or the most expensive in your class? The quality, the service, the support, the facilities, and the customer experience must parallel the pricing. If you have cheap infrastructure, you cannot be premium priced. If you have an expensive, high-class infrastructure, you cannot be, and do not want to be, the low-cost solution.

Whatever price you decide upon is not the final price. You need to take that pricing to the marketplace and certify it, because the market will ultimately determine if your price is realistic. If you lose every deal on price, then chances are your price is too high. Conversely, if nobody ever objects to your price, you are probably leaving some margin on the table. Go with your price for a few months. Make lots of calls as well as proposals, and then adjust according to what you learn in the market. That will be the ultimate price test. The marketplace is the ultimate judge of your price. Is the price appropriate for the quality of product or level of service that you are delivering to the marketplace? Meetings, discussions, studies, and analyses will allow you to determine your price schedule, but only success or failure in the market will ultimately determine if your strategy was correct.

If you are one of many in a particular industry, and you have a great number of competitors, your pricing options and strategies will be formed and limited by the competition. If you are in a newer business or technology that isn't mature, the pricing paradigm has not yet been formulated. My company was in the online data backup business in 1998, and we literally had no like competition. We were pioneering and competing against the older way of doing business, writing to tape and transferring the tapes off-site in a truck or having the company's office manager or IT director take the tapes home. There was no competitor to mimic, there was no standard pricing model, and we literally made it up as we went along.

As we will discuss later on in the chapter on differentiation, pricing is one of the ways to differentiate your company from the competition. The instinct for many newly minted entrepreneurs is to compete on price during the early days, and I certainly would endorse that. However, longer term I do not like the strategy of being the low-priced leader, as it is risky, and someone will always come along and beat your price. I actually like the opposite strategy of going with a high or higher price and becoming the premium provider. Many successful companies, from Coach to Nordstrom to BMW to Rolex, have competed most successfully as a premium quality product or service with a high price.

I feel that in every market or business, there is always a span of prices form low to mid to high to premium, and probably there are companies that are successful in each of those price niches. So there is no right or wrong answer here with regards to pricing. It is a matter of what you want your company to be, and how you want to position relative to all of your competitors. This is a big decision and one that is long term, so think it through thoroughly before you adopt your strategy.

This may sound like I am contradicting myself, but I am not. Once I have picked the pricing strategy and decided to be "premium priced," that does not mean that I never will discount or give early adopters a special introductory price. As I repeat over and over in this tome, getting your first five or ten or twenty clients is of paramount importance. It is hard, it is challenging, and it requires creativity and daring and a determination to succeed. If I give those early customers an introductory price to come on board, I really don't care if I am making money or profit on those early sales. It just doesn't matter; I need those clients. If you do give that customer a really attractive price, the customer may be concerned that you will substantially raise the price after the introductory price, as many companies have done that in the past. What I have done in this situation is to assure the customer, and write it in the contract, "your special price is $xx.xx for the first year, and after year one we will not raise your price by more that 10 percent in years two and three. This way the customer is protected and knows you are not trying to trick them and will be much more willing to do the deal with you.

As you build your pricing strategy, it is fluid and will change during your first year or two of business. You will not get it right on the very first try. One suggestion is to set your price high and come down if not appropriate. It is much easier to lower prices than it is to raise them. If you establish a low price strategy and it does not work, it is very difficult to go to your customers and prospects and raise the price.

In summary, decide where you want to be positioned in price: price leader, average price, a premium price, or expensive. Align your price with the image you want to project to your customers. Maintain flexibility and be willing to adjust the price based on market conditions and the competitive environment. Eventually, you will figure it out and build a price model that fits, and one that customers will be willing to pay and feel that they are getting the appropriate value. Like many things in business, pricing is an art as much as a science.

— CHAPTER THIRTEEN —

IF YOU THINK YOU WILL GET A BANK LOAN TO LAUNCH YOUR BUSINESS, THINK AGAIN

Many new or potential entrepreneurs think they will get a commercial bank loan to launch their business. I am telling you that that, unfortunately, is not going to happen. Banks, in good times, are risk adverse. In current times they are very risk adverse.

The bank has two major concerns when they lend money to a company.

One, how do they get repaid if the business thrives? What is the cash flow coverage versus the debt repayment? They generally want at least three times, sometimes more, coverage. So if you borrow $100,000 for three years, your monthly principal and interest payment will be approximately $4,000. Therefore, the bank will be looking for free cash flow of $12,000 to $20,000 per month to cover that debt repayment. Clearly, if you are a start-up, your monthly cash flow is *zero* at the beginning stages.

Two, how do they get repaid if the business is not successful? They want to see hard assets to secure the loan, which could be accounts receivables, equipment, hard assets, your house, personal guarantee, CDs or something that can be liquidated to recoup their investment in the event you fail. And make no mistake, if you fail and cannot repay the debt, they will take your house. So think very carefully about personal guarantees. Getting a personal bailout from the Obama administration to pay or forgive your debt is not likely.

It goes without saying that a new company probably has neither free cash flow to cover the debt repayment nor sufficient assets to secure the loan. So, bottom line, the likelihood of securing bank debt in your first year or two is remote.

Let me share a true story as to how I went about securing a $100,000 line of credit a few years ago. I was launching AmeriVault, my fourth company at the time. I approached a loan officer at the then Bank of Boston to discuss a loan. I had a very good track record as a serial entrepreneur and felt quite confident that this bank would be anxious to make me a loan. I had sold two companies previously and had a pretty strong personal financial statement. In fact, following the sale of a previous company, this very same bank had recruited me to their private banking group with the hopes of lending me money and managing my investment assets. I was just the type of prospect they savored—in my midforties, significant investments, strong balance sheet, no debt, plenty of funds to pay cash for college educations for my three children, etc.

They worked very hard to get me as a client, and, in fact, I did do business with the private banking group. So approaching that very same bank for a commercial loan a few years later seemed to be a slam-dunk, at least in my opinion. I went through the process with the loan officer, and the bottom line was they would not give me an unsecured line of credit for $100,000 because my company was a start-up with no track record of success. I reminded them that my previous companies had borrowed and repaid over $1,000,000 from a bank they acquired, and those banks had enjoyed a very good profit on all those loans. There was little or no risk with me due to my track record and the fact that I had some personal financial wealth as well.

I was wrong on all accounts. They would not do the deal unsecured, and I knew at that point no other commercial bank would view the request any differently. I did prevail, sort of. The only way the bank would make the loan was if I deposited $130,000 in a CD in their bank to secure the $100,000 line of credit. I reluctantly agreed to their terms, as I felt it was important for us to secure a line of credit and establish credit for AmeriVault. Several years later, we were able to borrow over $7,500,000 very easily from a different bank.

So a bank loan for a start-up company is nonexistent. Under no circumstances should you consider a loan as a source for start-up capital, or you will be very disappointed. If someone has told you you can get a loan, or if you have read another book on new companies getting low-interest loans, do not believe it. It is not going to happen. In my chapter on financing we will discuss multiple sources of capital for new companies, but bank debt will not be one of the options.

Your initial funding will have to come from other sources. Forget the bank loan unless you have significant assets or capital to secure the loan or purchase the CD, as I did. Commercial banks are just not risk-takers, and it is rare they will do business with a company that is less than two years old. Your start-up funds will have to come from personal savings, friends and family, angel investors, or venture capitalists. Don't even waste your time talking to the bank until you have a financial track record.

— Chapter Fourteen —

VCs May Be Good People, but They're Not Nice People

It takes money to make money. We have all heard that phrase, and it is, in fact, a truism. If you are launching a company, you need some start-up capital.

There are three choices to raise this capital:

- Bootstrap, self-fund
- Bootstrap, friends and family
- Institutional capital, venture capital, or angel network

I have done all three and have some strong opinions as I peer in the rearview mirror.

Different types of businesses require different amounts of capital. If you have the ability to self-bootstrap, *do it*. Sources of capital would be second mortgage, home-equity loan, 401k advance, life insurance loan, or your savings. Clearly, the benefit, if you can do it, is you own 100 percent of the stock, have no partners, and will never disappoint a friend or relative if things don't go according to plan.

By the way, bank debt is *not an option*. If you think you can go down to your hometown savings bank and get a 100k loan, you will be disappointed. You are a start-up and have no track record, and no bank will give you a loan, period. There is one way around this. I went to my local bank and asked for a 100k line of credit. I had many years of success (sold two earlier companies) and a significant net worth. Their private banking group had approached me years earlier to solicit me as a client because I had financial assets. The only way I could get the loan for a new start-up was to give them 130k in personal deposits. They, in turn, would use those assets to give me a line of credit. And, believe it or not, I did it. No regrets. Later I raised venture capital. If you can self-fund and not take in partners or investors, I would urge you to do so.

If you don't have the assets to self-fund or you need more capital than you have personally, the next option is friends and family. This option is where you solicit friends and family in the form of equity. They get stock or loans.

I prefer friends to family, as family and business are a tough combination. Thanksgiving dinner could be uncomfortable if your father-in-law invested in your company and things are not going well. At least with friends you don't see them on every holiday.

Most entrepreneurs go to family first, as the likelihood of getting help is usually greater, but the cost of failure is more painful.

In one of my companies, I got three golfing buddies to invest, and they took turns sitting on my board of directors and received regular financial statements to stay abreast of how the company was proceeding. I am pleased to report they all received an above-average return on their investment, and, most importantly, we are all still friends.

Lastly, there is the venture capital alternative. Venture capital comes in two flavors, organized angel groups and institutional venture capitalists.

Angel groups have grown up. They have become more organized and more professional and are doing a larger share of early-stage or start-up funding. Many VC firms are doing larger deals and later-stage deals, which create a vacuum in early stage that is being filled by angel groups (I belong to two such groups).

An angel group is a mix of successful people with assets. They are accredited investors and are usually successful, cashed-out entrepreneurs that have accumulated significant wealth. In addition to bringing capital to a company, they bring great experience and serve as board members, advisers, and mentors. They unselfishly provide expertise and guidance to the founders with the hopes of having a successful exit and return on investment. Although they clearly have a profit motive and are not investing for charitable purposes, I think for many the angel option is a far better solution than the institutional VC.

I have been solicited by over thirty-six VCs in the last several years, usually after I no longer needed the money. All of them, without fail, tell you how they are different and deliver so much more than capital. Those other things they bring usually include contacts, referrals, expertise, recruiting help, operational guidance, and introductions to service providers, and it all sounds wonderful. In reality, I have seen very little of this firsthand. Proceed based on the fact that you get the money, and anything else is a bonus but not a guarantee.

Another reason I have a built-in bias is that I have found the VCs are in it for themselves and care less about the founders, employees, customers, and suppliers of the company. I won't air the dirty laundry here but suffice to say I have numerous stories to substantiate these comments. Here's one example: I made my VCs $15,000,000 in profit and my lead partner never picked up the phone or visited me in person to say thank you after we closed the deal. He did send me a brief e-mail.

My last complaint about some but not all VCs is many of them have never been entrepreneurs or CEOs. The industry attracts many very bright people. Often they spend a couple of years at an investment banking house in an analyst role. They then go to a VC firm for a few years. Then they go off to graduate school to secure an MBA and return to a different VC firm with the promise of becoming a partner in a few years. So, they are very bright and usually can read a financial statement like most of us read a horoscope, but they have no real-world experience. They have never sold a customer, fixed a customer service issue, hired a sales manager, dealt with an IT issue, fired a nonperforming employee, done marketing or PR, or negotiated with a bank, all the things we need to deal with every day as company founders.

That does not make them bad people; it just limits their true value to you, the founder. But the main reason for engaging them is they bring capital, and that they do well.

Here's one last comment on VCs. Their main goal is to own over 51 percent of the company. That means you own less than 49 percent of the company, and they call the shots. When you first fund, if you have a good idea, a viable plan, and a good team, you will get funding, and you will be in control. If you go back to the well for additional capital (and almost everybody does) you will lose control, and the valuation will almost always put them in a majority ownership position. At that point, as a VC friend once warned me, they will tell you what kind of car to drive, how much you make, and how many hours a week you work. He was right.

VCs are *good* people and provide an invaluable resource to the entrepreneurial engine. They are just not, in many cases, *nice* people.

In summary, self-fund if you have the resources available to do so. If your company requires more capital than you have, pick your financial partners prudently.

— CHAPTER FIFTEEN —

MANAGING CASH FLOW

There are fewer things more important in a new business than managing cash. Start-up funding, as we discussed earlier, is hard to come by, particularly in a constrained economy. You will likely not be able to get a bank loan, and only one in fifty companies is successful in securing capital from institutional venture capitalists. If you did borrow from friends and family, Uncle Hymie will be watching you like a hawk and making holiday dinners uncomfortable. So, whatever amount of cash or credit you have to launch your business, treat it like the precious resource that it is.

Although there is not time to cover all of the cash-flow tricks of the trade, let me try to create a primer of some simple but effective tools you can employ during the early years.

Your payroll, coupled with employee benefits like health and dental insurance, will always be your biggest expense in business. You need quality people to ensure success, and you need to pay them competitively in order to recruit them. But an effective strategy might be to pay them at 80 percent of market rate and then give them extra stock options for ownership and assure them a significant raise once the company gets to positive cash flow.

Hire seniors who have retired from their first career but want to work part time. They can make a huge contribution. Perhaps, some of those early retirees are very comfortable financially and are in a position to work for equity, as they don't need the money. Or give them both stock and salary. You will be getting a proven veteran at very affordable dollars.

Pay your bills timely but not too timely. Stretching out accounts payables has always been an acceptable strategy for managing cash. When you make a purchase, negotiate terms or delayed payment with the vendor. You may be better off paying a higher price and paying over six months than getting a good discount with the requirement of paying in thirty days.

Collect accounts receivable with great discipline. Make it somebody's job and incent him or her for keeping your accounts receivable at a certain target, forty-four days DSO (days sales outstanding), as an example. If your last month's sales were 100k and your accounts receivable are 150k, then you have DSO of forty-five days, and this would generally be considered a good target for AR. Years ago, I gave my receptionist a quarterly and annual bonus for keeping the AR where we wanted it to be. It was a win/win, as I never had old receivables, and she consistently earned her bonus. It was a very good investment for our company.

If money is tight and payday comes, don't pay the owners. Not pleasant, but it happens to most entrepreneurs at some point in time. However, *never do this with the rest of your staff.* They need to be paid, and you need to keep them happy, motivated, and committed to the goal. Nothing dampens that spirit and enthusiasm like a missed payroll.

Barter is a wonderful thing. (See my earlier story about trading shoes for backup services) Bartering is a wonderful way to conserve cash. Trading your services for a copier or Web site design or accounting services is a creative way to get what you need while minimizing the cash outlay. There are many small and midsize companies that embrace barter. You just need to ask.

There are many companies failing due to the economic malaise. Their misfortune can be to your advantage. I have bought office furniture and partitions and equipment for several of my companies at a very deep discount. You can buy almost anything today on Ebay or other Web sites that specialize in selling everything you will need for your business.

Not only can you pay your employees with stock, but perhaps a major supplier or service provider (lawyer, accountant, and marketing consultant) will take their fees in stock rather than cash. I would do this selectively, but it can be a wise decision, and it also commits these people to making sure they do everything to assure your success.

Get a favorable lease. Landlords usually prefer to give a few months free rent rather than discount the rent. If you can rent an office and not pay rent for up to six months (probably your second biggest expense after payroll) this is a huge help to managing your cash flow. The real estate market is quite soft in many parts of the country, and it is a great time to aggressively negotiate a favorable lease for your start-up company.

Defer purchases that are not absolutely critical. We have *needs* and we have *wants*. There is a huge difference. You *need* an office, business cards, a logo, a computer system, a Web site, and e-mail. You *want* team shirts, a 401k, a trade show booth, and fancy new office furniture. The *wants* must be delayed until the cash flow is no longer an issue for your growing company.

Manage cash and do it with great discipline. Running out of cash is the number one reason for business failure. Start early and develop this discipline, and it will pay dividends for you and contribute to your success.

— Chapter Sixteen —

Managing Cash Is
Like Flying a Boeing 747

Cash flow, positive cash flow, that is, may be the single largest challenge for newly minted entrepreneurs. Positive cash flow is having more cash coming in than you have going out for expenses. Getting to positive cash flow in your start-up life is a huge step— like first communion, college graduation, your wedding day, and the birth of your first child. But getting to positive cash flow, sometimes like marriage or a birth, can happen more than once. The reason is that the path to business success often resembles a set of stairs rather than the slow, gently growing curve.

You get to positive cash, and then you buy a big asset or hire a new sales manager or buy some furniture, and bang, back to negative cash. But that's okay, because that's what it is like growing a business.

So let me share with you my 747 analogy. I have used it for years and shared it with many an entrepreneur I have counseled. Once, shortly after September 11, I was on an airplane from Boston to Miami, and there were, literally, four passengers on board. There were more crew than passengers, but they flew the flight anyway. Whether there were four passengers or 252 passengers, you need a full crew, pay all the gate fees, use almost as much fuel, and have the same wear and tear on the airplane.

Bottom line, it costs the airline the same dollars whether the flight is nearly full or nearly empty.

In any business, you have a certain amount of fixed overhead, payroll, rent, utilities, insurance, etc. Those expenses, not unlike flying a Boeing747, are fixed, and as a result are part of your monthly expenses regardless of your sales level in any given month. So, once you put that 747 up, or in your world pay your fixed monthly nut, you can accept additional sales at lower margins. A sale at lower margins contributes to paying expenses and is always better than no sale at all.

I don't adhere to discounting consistently, but sometimes it is prudent in order to secure a large new account or accept a big project at lower margins than normal, as it is just like putting one more body in that half-empty airplane.

This applies to salespeople as well. If a salesperson came to me towards the end of the month and wanted to discount the price in order to get a new account, I may be more apt to say yes if we were having a slow month as opposed to if we were having a very robust month. Sometime, getting more sales, just like more bodies in an airplane, can be the difference between positive cash flow and negative cash flow in your start-up business. I don't want to start a culture of consistent discounting but think about the 747, periodically; it makes sense.

— Chapter Seventeen —

Debt Is Always
Cheaper Than Equity

So far I have ripped venture capitalists for the way they treat their portfolio companies' entrepreneurs. I also told you to forget about getting a bank loan, as it will not happen for a start-up. Now I am telling you that debt is cheaper than equity, and, given the choice, you should choose debt over equity. Yes, all these thoughts are correct.

So what exactly does this mean? When you sell equity or stock in your company to investors, it is pretty much until death does us part, forever or an exit, whichever comes first. Not only do those investors have ownership, but also they will probably want to express an opinion and may even want to take a somewhat active role in the running of the business. Entrepreneurs generally do not like this and started a company because they want to call the shots, not answer to someone else.

Debt or a loan is much cleaner and better. When a company secures a loan, whether it is from a bank or from individuals, it is a temporary situation that terminates once the loan is repaid. Interest rates are historically cheap, so don't worry about the rate you pay, as it is negligible in the long term and is deductible to boot. And the lender is not receiving part ownership in the company. As a founder one goal you will have is to maintain as much ownership of your company for as long as you can. Getting a loan, versus selling stock, allows you to do that.

You may ask, "How do I know whether I should select debt or sell stock in my business?" Here are two tips:

One, you need to be able to repay the loan on a consistent basis. If you have some cash flow and can repay the loan consistently, this is a better choice. Also, you may write the note so the interest or principle, or both, are deferred for the first year or two until you do generate consistent cash flow. If it will take a long time to generate positive cash flow because you are developing a product or writing software, then equity is a much better way to go.

Two, if you need the money to buy a piece of equipment or hire a sales rep., etc., which will have an immediate impact on increasing sales, debt is the better alternative. For example, if I run a copy center, and buying a bigger, faster copier with debt or leasing will allow me to take on a new law firm account that will result in immediate revenue, then borrow the money.

Alternatively, if you are funding negative cash flow, and it is taking longer than anticipated to get to profitability (remember I told you to double the number in an earlier chapter), and it will, I would be more apt to find some shareholders to invest in the company, as the payback will be much longer.

You will need cash to fund the business. Most of us don't have an Uncle Hymie to write the check (I certainly didn't) and need to go outside to fund-raise. And if you do have an Uncle Hymie, he probably wants a return on his investment.

Look at the amount of money you need and what you will do with it. Ask such questions as, will it have a short-term impact on sales? How long will it take to pay it back? You can then make the decision on whether a loan or stock sales would most benefit you and the company.

- Calculate break even and double it
- Find an angel, *not* a bank
- A bank loan is not an option in the early days
- Avoid the VCs if you can
- Ferociously manage and preserve your cash
- Given the choice, debt is better than equity

— CHAPTER EIGHTEEN —

HIRE GREAT PEOPLE

Sound easy? It's not. I know this advice seems like common sense, but sometimes common sense is not so common.

Recruiting and hiring top people on a consistent basis is as much art as it is science, and it takes work. There are so many pitfalls in the hiring process, and no matter how deliberate and thorough you are, mistakes can be made. I employed an interview process whereby the candidate interviewed with three groups of three, each group being from a different department. The groups typically have a cross section of departments—sales, technical, administrative, marketing, human resources, etc. Each interview should last forty-five to sixty minutes, with everyone participating in the process. Additionally, I utilize a personality profile system from Predictive Index and do significant reference checking as well. This system is a reliable process that usually results in finding and hiring the best candidates. However, no system is bulletproof.

In building a leadership team, the company needs a core group of three to seven people to build the company around. With a company comprised of ten employees, the team can be made up of three people. With eighty to one hundred employees, that team should comprise six or seven.

Even with a comprehensive recruitment process, not everyone you hire will be a rock star. The key is: your *top team* must be the best. If the leadership team and key midmanagers, or individual contributors, are all rock stars the rest of the workforce can be average and your annual turnover won't hurt you. The core group (10 to15 percent of your total head-count) will carry the day and drive the business to success.

The Internet has changed many industries in the last decade, but it may have impacted the recruiting industry as much or more than most. There are hundreds of job Web sites and job boards that have made access to talented people far easier and cheaper than in years past. Sites have become extremely targeted so you can find precisely the people you want with a very specific expertise.

At the risk of alienating the professional recruiters, I profess there is absolutely no reason for you to use a recruiter or recruiting company today to find your top people. To a great extent, I feel this industry has been made obsolete by the Internet, and you can do everything the recruiter will profess they do for you without them. Traditional recruiters can charge from 15 percent to 30 percent of the candidate's first-year compensation, so you will be facing a fee of over $30,000 to recruit a senior team member. This is an expense you do not need and cannot afford during your first year of business.

I have hired over three hundred people in my career, and as you can tell, I have developed a bias against recruiters. My apologies to anyone reading this book that is a member of the recruiter community; don't take it personally. You, as the business owner, can do everything that the recruiter is doing for you. Finding qualified candidates is the most important part of the process, and the Internet job sites have made that easy and affordable. Screening those resumes is a time-consuming process and clearly a very important part of the hiring process.

But the big job sites, Monster, Career Builder, and Hot Jobs, and lots of smaller, more specialized sites, have become sophisticated enough that you can search and only get resumes that closely meet your requirements. If you write the job description and company requirements well enough, you will save a lot of time and effort by reading only resumes that are qualified for your needs.

It is most important to see the candidates in person. Reading a resume can be a screen for requirements, but it is just not the same as spending forty-five minutes in person with that candidate. I have (and I am not alone) been enamored by a resume only to be very unimpressed with the candidate once I met him or her in person. Conversely, I have accepted an average resume and invited the candidate in and been blown away by the candidate in person. It is time-consuming, but get as many candidates as you can for interviews and don't rely on reading resumes or e-mails.

Recruiting and hiring is one of the most important things you do as an entrepreneur. It is as much art as science, and you will make good choices and some bad choices. The bad choices become obvious in fairly short order. When you do make a bad choice, fix it quickly and dismiss that person and go find the right one.

Lastly, fully check references before making the hire. It is surprising how many companies fail at this and don't bother to check references. This reference checking, done correctly, can reveal things about the candidate that you just will not uncover in the interview process. Do not shortchange the reference process, as it is one of the most important steps in the process.

As I will state repeatedly in this book, getting the best possible team of people is job one. There will be many challenges, disappointments, setbacks, losses, and big problems in the next few years at your start-up company. A great, committed team of people will be necessary to get through all of that and continue on the path to success.

Final thought on people. You will work some very long hours in your new business. You will probably spend more time with some of your early employees than you will spend with your family. You will get to know these people really well and establish a special bond with many of them. It is important to hire people that you like, people who have a sense of humor and people you can get along with. Do not hire jerks. More common sense here, but it is important common sense. Sometimes people are very talented and could make a contribution, but they are just jerks. Write yourself a note: don't hire jerks.

— CHAPTER NINETEEN —

MAKE THEM OWNERS

Every new business owner faces the decision early on whether to make the employees owners or to hold all the stock individually. It is a difficult decision, and one that has several factors to consider.

If you are building a lifestyle business and plan to keep the company a long time, perhaps hire your kids someday, then do not share ownership with others. If, on the other hand, your goal is to grow the company quickly and be acquired or do an initial public offering, *I would absolutely recommend you share ownership with others.*

The decision then becomes the question of, do I want to incentivize my key management team or do I want every employee in the company to participate? If you do an approved stock ownership plan, you cannot discriminate, and you must include all staff members in the plan.

I have done all of the above and found having an IRS-approved stock plan, which included all of our employees, to be a very good thing. Some of the reasons for this are as follows:

- Treat them as owners; spend your money like it is your own, because it is.
- Act like an owner, because you are.

- We are all in this together, and we will have a payday, so let's work really hard as a team for our mutual benefit, not just the founders' benefit.
- It sends a good message to our customers.
- It builds camaraderie.
- It rewards longtime employees for their devotion, loyalty, hard work, and results.

Recently, when I sold our company, it was very rewarding for me, personally, to see several of our early team reap a nice financial reward. For many, it was the largest check of their careers. It is a special feeling for the individual and for the founders as well.

There is a flip side to this thinking. Stock options or shares could be a demotivator if, at times, the value of the option is underwater. This has happened a lot in the past several years as the market tumbled to historic lows. In these cases the employees may feel that ownership is not a perk or benefit and they are getting no value for the options. This results in the ownership becoming a negative and certainly doesn't work as intended.

Finally, there are ways to extend the ownership benefit to just the key team with phantom shares and other tools that do allow an owner to discriminate. The theory is that if we reward the leadership team, they will be responsible to motivate the balance of the workforce. I feel this is a very good option. As I wrote earlier, motivate the few, and they will lead the many.

There is no right or wrong answer on this subject. It is a personal choice for the entrepreneur to make but one that is worthy of much thought and consideration before making the final decision.

— Chapter Twenty —

Non-compete and
Confidentiality Agreements

Non-compete agreements and, to a lesser extent, confidentiality or nondisclosure agreements, are a controversial subject. I get asked all the time about non-compete agreements by entrepreneurs. Questions include such things as: Should I have my employees sign them? Are they enforceable? Do I need to give my people consideration if I ask them to sign one?

Let me say right up front that I am not an attorney (and you should definitely consult one when you do this), so my views are strictly as a business guy.

If you have a stock option plan and are sharing ownership in the company with employees, I would have them sign non-compete agreements. In many states, in order to make the non-compete agreement legal and enforceable, you must give consideration to the person signing the agreement, and that is most often in the form of stock or stock options.

It is much easier to sell the non-compete early in the company's formation and at the time of hiring your employees. If you go to people after they have been with the company for a few years and ask them to sign a non-compete, it becomes more difficult and can raise a lot of questions. Do it at the point that you write a stock option plan. Both of these steps often accompany a fund-raising event with venture or angel investors.

If you are starting a lifestyle company or are not raising a significant amount of start-up capital, I would forego the non-compete agreement. I would, however, ask the staff to sign a *confidentiality* or *nondisclosure* agreement. This document states that you will keep all company information confidential and not disclose information such as trade secrets, customer lists, budgets, or payroll information with people outside of the company. This just makes good business sense and should not offend anyone who is asked to sign it. It also gives you and the company some limited protection should an employee leave and go to work for a competitor.

At some point in your entrepreneurial life, you will have a key employee leave and start a competing company or go to work for a competitor. It happens to all of us, and it will happen to you. When it does happen, the existence of a non-compete agreement may allow you to stop it. The existence of a confidentiality agreement may stop the person from sharing confidential information about your company with the new employer.

Many employers, once they find out someone is bound by a non-compete, will merely pass on that candidate rather then get embroiled in potential litigation. I have sent companies a nasty, legal-sounding letter informing them that my former employee is under a non-compete. That is often enough of a threat to convince them to move forward with a different candidate.

These few points deal with the defensive or perhaps negative consequences of the non-compete and confidentiality agreements. However, there is a positive spin as well.

As I have said repeatedly, a talented and motivated workforce is your most critical asset. Getting people committed to the company and feeling pride of ownership is necessary for success. Ownership in the company is the number one motivator. Tying together ownership and non-compete builds motivation and a sense of pride.

All of these things are a big decision and should not be taken lightly and will impact you and your company in a very significant way. Seek out professional advice and weigh the pluses and minuses, and then decide what the best course of action is for your company.

Chapter Twenty-One

Culture: Build It or Just Get It?

You hear a lot today about company culture, but where does that culture come from? Does the entrepreneur create it, does it just happen, or is it a combination of the two?

In my view it is some of each. We build cultures by the way we hire, the way we operate, the way we dress, and with our ideas. Basically, it's the way we conduct ourselves on a day-to-day basis. A culture gets birthed by the founder and the very early hires. You need to decide if you are a relaxed, laid-back work environment or a button-down, more disciplined company or something in between. Giving your people responsibility for making decisions, in my view, is one of the most important things one can do in developing the culture. The type of people you hire and their personality type will be a major factor in that developing culture. Little things matter, such as having a basketball hoop in the office or an air hockey game, social functions, and company lunches, to name a few.

Not all founders are good at the culture stuff, and that is okay. If you are not good at this, one of your early hires needs to be. Take the bubbly, fun, upbeat employee and make that person VP of fun. Give him or her the time, the permission, and the budget to have some funs things, and start to build that early company culture. Just having a cookout in the parking lot for Friday lunch or beers and burgers after hours some day is a great way to get started. But someone needs to be in charge of fun, and there will likely be someone among your first six hires that is good at this and would love to do it, Just identify that person early and have some fun.

A long-standing tradition in my last company was that our normal business casual dress code became relaxed during the summer season from Memorial Day to Labor Day. Our staff was welcome to wear shorts and jeans on a daily basis, not just on Fridays, as we did the rest of the year. The exception to that rule was that if we were hosting a guest, usually a customer or prospect, an e-mail would go out a couple of days in advance asking that people dress business casual on that day. This was very popular with all of our staff and was a central part of our culture.

For some reason, our new owners recently decided this was a bad idea and eliminated the perk. To pour salt into the wound, a couple of tech guys were sent home and charged with a half-day vacation when they showed up in shorts on a hot summer day. It only goes to show that really smart people (our new owners, not the tech guys) can do really dumb things. When it comes to keeping your staff highly motivated, company culture ranks right up there with salary and benefits. Your culture develops early and lasts a long time. Don't allow it to just happen, but work hard to affect the positive culture that will nurture success.

Allow me to brag about something we did early-on in our company to establish our company culture. I talk about this elsewhere in the book under motivating employees, but more than anything it helped to craft our early corporate culture. We took the whole damn company to Bermuda for a long three-day weekend. Sure, there were only eight employees at the time, including the two co-founders, but the company paid for the whole trip. I will tell you the details later on, so I don't want to repeat them here. Suffice to say, this one event in our early years did more than anything else to bring our people and their families closer together and craft our culture for many years to come.

Culture is important to a company, and the earlier you get it launched, the better off you will be. Make it happen on purpose, not by accident.

— CHAPTER TWENTY-TWO —

PERFORM PERSONNEL
REVIEWS RELIGIOUSLY

Hiring great people is very important in building a company. After you *get* them you need to *keep* them. But, more importantly, you need to keep them highly motivated each and every day.

Personnel reviews are very important in motivation. I have always been a zealot when it comes to insisting that all personnel reviews be done precisely when they are *supposed* to be done. Employees know their anniversary date and know their review date. In our company we always evaluated our people two times per year, the first being a performance review and the second a financial review, at which time the employee can expect an increase.

Managers receive an e-mail from the human resource department informing them as to which of their staff members are to receive their semiannual or annual review during the upcoming month. The manager is held accountable for completing that review in a timely and thorough manner.

One of my companies was acquired by a Fortune 500 company. That company lacked discipline in the review process. I am convinced that this lack of discipline in granting timely reviews led to the deterioration of morale among the employees. I have talked to several of my former staff members who attest that a lack of timely reviews was the single contributing factor to that deterioration.

Personnel reviews are very easy to do, and they are *critically* important. I urge you to start on day one with this commitment; make sure your people are reviewed on a timely basis. By the way, you will be doing all the reviews yourself in the early days, so there are no excuses if they don't get done. You cannot pass the buck. Do this from day one, and it will return a great dividend.

Attracting and hiring the very best people is, as I have said before, the single most important factor in building a successful company. You work very hard and spend money and resources to find them. You go through a comprehensive screening process to evaluate them. So make sure once you get them on board to treat them right in order to keep them and to keep their morale at the very highest level.

There are many surveys that have been done that indicate what is most important to employees in their job satisfaction. Their net pay or compensation is usually number four or five in importance, while other things, like recognition, team effort, benefits and promotion, are far more important. Quite often little things that take very little time and effort on the part of the owners or managers can have a huge impact on the positive morale of the troops, and this is most important. Motivated, loyal employees will pull you through those tough challenges that come up in every new company. Do the little things, including the consistent and timely reviews for your team members.

— Chapter Twenty-Three —

Over-communicate

Recently, I was at a cookout talking to a person about what they do and about their company. As I often do, I quizzed the person about the company and the type of business they were in. I was amazed to learn that even though he had been with the company for over six years, he knew very little about what they did, their size in terms of revenue, and/or whether they were profitable and growing. This has happened to me on many occasions. I find it most surprising that a great many people who have worked for companies for several years know as little as they do about their company's business. It would seem to me that if your family's future and well-being rested on your company, you would want to know how the company was doing financially, and if your job was secure in the future. We are in a stressed economy today, and a great many companies are down 25 percent or more from previous times. Now, more than ever, it is critical to communicate to the team how the company is doing. I have made thousands of sales calls over my career and often open the conversation by asking the attendees in the meeting how long they have been with the business and asking if they would educate me regarding the business. I just cannot believe the level of people's naïveté when it comes to their company. They spend over a third of their waking hours at the business and yet know relatively little about the company. This is usually the fault of the company, as opposed to the fault of the individual.

We have all heard the importance of good communication in any relationship. Whether it is with your spouse, siblings, parent, child, neighbor, or co-worker, we have been trained that good communication matters. Yet many companies do a lousy job of communicating with their workers.

As an entrepreneur, I urge you not just to communicate, but also to over-communicate. When someone comes on board, or preferably before they join the company, share the dream, the goal, and the value proposition with them. Take the time to share exactly what you are doing, what business you are in, why you feel you will be successful, and, importantly, what you expect the individual to contribute to the overall effort. This shouldn't just happen when you are interviewing or when someone is new on board, but continuously. Have formal *and* informal, lunchroom and water cooler sessions to continuously inform everyone what and how the company is doing.

I personally consider everyone in my companies to be in sales, so I have always made an effort to train them on our value proposition so they could make apitch to a total stranger. That mini-pitch would include such things as what we do, why it is important, and what makes us good at it. It is not that I expect everyone to make sales calls, because I don't, but I feel better knowing that everyone in the company could do it if they were called upon. If a prospect for your product or service was at a cookout, as I explained above, and was in the market for your service, you just may get a customer if your employee communicated clearly and professionally what their company did when asked by a stranger. If all employees can make that brief sales pitch to a stranger, they will know precisely what we do and increase their own personal sense of pride and ownership.

It may sound trite and overused, but you need to communicate early and often, and educate and inform your people. It will make a difference.

— Chapter Twenty-Four —

Share the Numbers

I rambled on in an earlier chapter about employees that have been with the company for six years and know little or nothing about the company and its business. Those same employees would have no clue as to the financial well-being of the company and how they are doing with respect to sales and profits. As I have offered, this may not be the fault of the employee but rather the fault of the leadership.

Not only do I want you to educate, but I want you to take that a step further and discuss the monthly or quarterly financials with all of the troops.

A few years ago, Paul, a talented but somewhat introverted tech guy, walked into my office at six o'clock on a Friday night and asked if he could talk with me for a few minutes. I said sure and invited him in for a seat and a chat. The company was doing very well at the time and was highly profitable. We posted all of the current month's new sales on a white board in the office and were having a slow month. It was summer, and that is to be expected. Paul told me he had been watching the tote board and was concerned and asked me if he should be looking for a new job. I assured him we were fine, business was good, and we valued his contribution and would be disappointed if he left.

Driving home that evening I made a decision to be much more open with our financials and to share revenue and profit information with the entire company on a monthly basis. We posted results in the cafeteria and talked about it on a regular basis. Subsequent to that we put an all-company incentive in place tied to our financial success, and everyone became much more interested in how we were doing. Paul never came in again on a Friday night to express his concern and continues to be a motivated and committed team member of the company.

There are three ways to share this information, and I will leave it up to each individual reader what is best for your company. The important thing to remember is that an educated and enlightened employee is more committed and loyal than one who is kept in the dark.

Share the revenue numbers on a monthly basis. This is probably the best way to go during the early years. It is simple, and you are probably bleeding cash, which is far more difficult for most to understand. Sharing the monthly sales number will demonstrate progress and show that the company is making progress and that the team has a secure future.

Share the revenue and bottom-line number on a routine basis. It doesn't have to be monthly in the beginning. Perhaps quarterly is better, as it will give you more time to gain traction each time you share the numbers.

Finally, share all with everyone on a regular basis. If you do this it is clearly more work and needs adequate preparation so you present in a fashion that everyone understands. You could either share the full P&L statement or a summary document that shows major categories of revenue and expenses.

You may also decide to share in-depth numbers with your key team (managers and supervisors) and share summary information with the entire workforce.

The one caveat is once you start to share you cannot go backwards and stop sharing. So if the company is not doing well, *everybody in the company knows*. If the company is not doing well, morale may suffer. If the trend continues, you may have your people out looking for jobs elsewhere.

Nobody said this was going to be easy. The failure rate of new start-up companies is high, and you need to perform at the highest level in order to succeed. So I do suggest that you share financial results with the company team members, but think it through thoroughly. You may want to wait until you have some successes in your pocket before educating all on the financial status of the company.

Chapter Twenty-Five

Incentive Compensation for All

Incentive compensation, also known as variable compensation, is commission or bonus paid to an employee for reaching a particular goal. We all know that it is common to pay salespeople a commission based on what they sell. Incentive compensation, at least in smaller or start-up companies, is rare.

I would urge you to consider utilizing incentive compensation in your company. There are two ways to do this. One, reward a small group, such as top managers, or, two, reward *everyone in the company*. I won't recommend one option over the other, as I feel both are productive. I would suggest that you at least consider this even in a start-up situation.

Generally, incentive compensation is tied to revenue and profits. For example, if you achieved a sales goal of $1,000,000 in revenue in your first year of business, perhaps a bonus of $50,000 is shared by all in the bonus pool. Incentives are a powerful motivator, and people are motivated by money but also by the self-satisfaction of attaining a group goal. At my company last year, everyone in the company (forty-five employees) shared in a bonus pool, and it was a great motivator. The concept for including everyone is that everyone makes a contribution, from the receptionist who answers the phone, to the tech that installs, to the accountant who bills, to the marketing manager that writes the press release, etc.

Alternately, in the early days, you may rather wish to incent only the senior management team. That team might include the CEO, CFO, VP of sales, and the tech or operations VP. The concept is that you motivate the key players, and it becomes their responsibility to motivate everyone on each of their teams. I think this approach can be just as effective and may be more affordable in the early years of your business. As you continue to grow you can expand the bonus pool to include others and ultimately to include everyone.

One of the most successful incentive plans I have ever conducted took place in the early years at AmeriVault. We had eight employees at the time and were starting to get some traction in the marketplace in the Northeastern United States. We set what I felt was a very aggressive goal and had a meeting with the entire company to announce the plan. It was midsummer, and if we reached our sales goal by December 31st, I would take the entire company to Bermuda for a long weekend the following spring. I have never in my career seen a group more cohesive and more motivated than our team of eight over those next five months. It was extraordinary, and we made our goals with room to spare.

While in Bermuda we decided to change the name of the company from Recovery Solutions to AmeriVault. Ultimately, this became a great benefit of our Bermuda adventure. AmeriVault went on to become one of the best-known brand names in our industry for years to come.

A few tips on incentive compensation and contests.

- The goal needs to be believable and achievable.
- It should be for a defined period.
- You need to report and *display* monthly progress.
- You must have meetings regularly to share results.
- Celebrate large customer wins.

- Recognize all the players and their contributions.
- Pay off timely, and celebrate the success.

Incentive compensation, either for all or for your core leadership group, is a viable strategy for young companies. I would heartily recommend this for your company, maybe not on day one but within the early years.

But I can't afford it, you may argue. Remember, you are only writing the checks if you attain the goal, and if the goal is significant enough it will provide sufficient profits and cash that you really *can* afford it. So don't use this as an excuse. It may just get you to that goal far faster than you might have done otherwise.

— CHAPTER TWENTY-SIX —

OUTSOURCING KEY ROLES

I have preached repeatedly about the importance of attracting great people to build a world-class company. In the early days, you need several key roles but may not be able to afford to hire them when you need them. There are alternatives.

Day one the founder or CEO will probably be the leader. You will likely also be the VP of sales and perhaps the CFO. Chances are you are not skilled at these three different roles and will need to hire others to take on these jobs as the company grows.

There are companies and accomplished individuals that perform these duties on a part-time basis. You certainly will not need a full-time CFO during your first two years of business, nor can you afford one, but you could outsource this need in the early days. You would contract with a company to provide a part-time CFO, perhaps one to two days per week, to oversee all financial functions and start to build a system and internal controls to deal with good accounting and finance principles. Today, you can hire virtually any role on this basis—HR, sales, financial, software development, operations, R&D, VP engineering, and on and on. You can also hire these same people temp to perm, which means they are temps in the early going, but if you have a great chemistry, you may hire them permanently, paying a fee of course, once you know the fit is good. I like temp to perm, as it allows you to get to know the candidate before inviting him or her to join the team on a permanent basis. Having to dismiss a senior team member after just a few weeks or months is a very challenging task, and one I would not wish on anyone. Temp to perm minimizes the likelihood of that happening.

Alternately, you could look for seniors who have a deep skill set but perhaps have financial resources and would only like to work one to three days per week. In the current economic climate there are thousands of senior managers who fit this role and may have taken early retirement or a package from their previous employer. They want to work, would love being part of a young company, and can make a great contribution, but they are no longer interested in climbing the corporate ladder. I would consider this pool of very available and talented people as one of the greatest resources currently available to young companies. I would urge you to seek them out. There are, I am sure, available Web sites for searching for this type of employee.

Lastly, there are many who would like to work part time. In many cases, those people have family obligations, young children or older parents that require them to work less than a forty-hour workweek. Many of them could hold the same job for a very long time in your company and be very reliable and make a great contribution. I would urge you to consider this type of candidate as well.

When building your team, it pays to think outside the box. Sure, we normally think in terms of full-time employees who work a traditional forty-hour workweek, but there are a great many other options, particularly for more senior positions.

Be creative. Finding and hiring the best team will bring success and pay dividends.

— Chapter Twenty-Seven —

Ego Is a Good
and a Bad Thing

Entrepreneurs are a different breed. They need to be self-assured, confident, have an attitude, and be a type-A personality in order to succeed. However, *ego* can be either a good or a bad thing, and one needs to keep his or her ego in check to assure success.

I have said previously that securing your first five to ten customers is one of the most critical steps to success. Without customers, there is no business. Any prospect you talk to will want to know who your customers are, how many you have, and how long they have been with you. Nobody wants to be first. Offering up some credible references is a necessary step to securing new clients. You cannot just say that you are better than their current vendor or that your service is better or that your pricing is less or that your quality is superior. You must prove it. One great way to do that is with testimonials or references.

In the start-up sales process, ego is a necessary asset. I always believed that by providing the highest quality data backup, we were doing well by our customers and literally "saving lives." I know our customer was much better off and more secure than they had been before they became our client. I felt it, I knew it, and I communicated it with great sincerity and credibility. One needs to have a pretty big ego to do that successfully but without being perceived as *arrogant*. There is a very fine line between ego and arrogance, and crossing that line can spell failure. Nobody wants to do business with an arrogant individual whose sense of his or her self-value is inflated beyond where it naturally belongs.

Conversely, when dealing with employees, partners, suppliers, and service providers, I suggest humility as the best approach. Let's zero in on employee relations. A manager or leader will not get the best and most out of his or her staff if that leader has an oversized ego and always has to offer up the answer. The staff will not be developed or motivated to come up with the appropriate answer on their own. A good leader develops the staff to make decisions and come up with answers on their own. This offers up growth in the individual as well as the business. An oversized ego on the part of the boss will not foster that type of growth. The boss must minimize his or her self-worth in order to build the team and the business.

Thus, is this confusing or illuminating? Hopefully it needs to be one or the other. A strong ego is an asset at the right time and in the right circumstance but is a liability in other circumstances. Figure out the difference between those two and enlarge or diminish your own self-importance and ego when the situation necessitates it. Everyone will win.

Bud's Bottom Line Takeaways

- Hire the best people on the planet
- Make them owners so they act like owners
- Every company has a culture so build yours
- Complete personnel reviews rigorously
- Tell your people everything, including financials
- Incent for success
- Keep your ego in check

— CHAPTER TWENTY-EIGHT —

INTRAPRENEUR IS A HOAX

Several years ago, someone coined the word "*intrapreneur*." This was an entrepreneur *inside a large company* who was doing the things that entrepreneurs do. Clever idea, but it is ill-conceived. There are numerous flaws in this concept.

- Entrepreneurs quit their real jobs; the other guys don't.
- Entrepreneurs work for free, often drawing little or no salary or expenses for several months; the other guys continue to get their salaries while they are entrepreneuring.
- Entrepreneurs very often get a second mortgage or home equity loan to finance and bootstrap the company's early days; the other guys get money from the mother ship.
- Entrepreneurs run the risk of alienating family, golf buddies, neighbors, or their father-in-law if the start-up is not successful (that's real motivation to succeed). Intrapreneurs don't disappoint anyone except maybe their boss.
- Entrepreneurs go out and recruit, hire, and train total strangers to bet their company on. Intrapreneurs grab the first couple of staff from the corporation.

- Entrepreneurs create a vision for the new company and what it looks like. Intrapreneurs go to the corporate strategy department for ideas.
- Entrepreneurs work unreasonable hours and miss the kid's soccer games and dance recitals, as we talked about earlier. Intrapreneurs never miss a game or dance because of work.
- Entrepreneurs are unemployed, depressed, and broke if they fail. Intrapreneurs have none of those consequences.

Are you beginning to get the idea? There is very little similarity between the *entrepreneur* and the *intrapreneur*. It just doesn't happen.

I have yet to see a survey that compares the relative success of these two groups, but I would be willing to bet the entrepreneurs win the race and kick the butts of the corporate guys. You have to have skin in the game to be successful, and absolutely nobody has more skin in the game than the entrepreneur who quits his job to chase his or her dream. I'll bet on that jockey any day.

I am not totally against this intrapreneur concept. It does have some merits.

It fosters the entrepreneurial spirit and gives people the chance to do it with a safety net in place.

It provides a dress rehearsal for an individual to do it on somebody else's dime. That person may later do it the "real way" and go out on his own to chase that dream. Having done it once and made the mistakes, no doubt that individual has a better chance of success when he does it the second time around.

It fosters innovation and creates new ideas and new jobs, at least for a time.

If you work for a larger company and are ever offered the opportunity to be the intrapreneur, grab it, especially if you have fostered ideas of someday starting your own business. As I have said above, this opportunity could be your dress rehearsal for the real thing later on in life. You will face many of the challenges and have many of the successes of a real entrepreneur without having to worry that the bank will take your house if you fail. It is a great opportunity and only comes along to a relatively few, so if you are presented the opportunity, I would urge you to consider it strongly.

— CHAPTER TWENTY-NINE —

THE GLASS MUST
BE HALF FULL

It goes without saying that you must have a positive attitude
if you're about to launch a business. It is, after all, one of the
most demanding and challenging endeavors that you will ever
undertake. *Attitude* is everything.

There will be many disappointments and setbacks. Things
just never happen quite the way we plan them. Earlier I advised
you to double the time and double the money you will need
to get to break-even. Regardless of how well you have planned,
much of what is involved in starting a company is outside of your
control. Prospects will disappoint, lenders will disappoint, your
staff will disappoint. Things that you are sure will happen on
time this week, will probably not, and may not happen at all.

Not all individuals are cut out for the role of entrepreneur.
Earlier I assembled a list of many of the qualities one must possess
to be an entrepreneur. Starting a company is one of the hardest
things you will do in your entire life. The disappointments will
far outstrip the successes in number over the first couple of years.
Additionally, as the boss, you need to fake it until you make it
and put on the positive attitude for your other employees when
they need it. I just cannot state too often how much your attitude
will contribute to your success or failure.

You need perseverance, you need willpower, you need to be able to handle disappointment and bounce back. Each and every day will be difficult. If you don't have the ability to be positive and see the glass as half full, rather than half empty, you will fail. Sounds simple, yet it may be more important than anything else you do.

— CHAPTER THIRTY —

DEALING WITH THE UNEXPECTED

One of the joys of being an entrepreneur is that things are ever changing and there are always new challenges to deal with on a daily basis. Many of those obstacles or challenges will not go in your favor, and many times things happen that are out of your control. How you deal with disappointment, how you cope, how you rebound, and how you refuse to quit is critical for success. It's easy to become discouraged following a setback. It takes grit to bounce back, to keep the faith, and to see the glass as half full when it is simultaneously half empty.

I would like to share a story that hopefully will provide encouragement to all aspiring entrepreneurs. My second business was DataVault, a company that stored records and data in a very secure environment for other companies. We were competing with not one, but two, very large competitors. We needed a compelling and competitive advantage. I decided I wanted to find and develop an underground Nike missile site. I was determined I could and *would* turn a missile site into an underground fortress to protect data. It would be a site far more secure than the above-ground buildings utilized by the two large competitors.

There were numerous sites of this type in the Northeast corridor that were built in the 1950s to protect the eastern shore against attack. They housed Nike missiles, which were ground-to-air missiles that could take out an approaching attack from the enemy. Most of these sites were mothballed in the late '50s and early '60s by the Department of Defense and were sold or donated to area towns or sold to individuals. Most were not utilized for any productive purpose, but some, in fact, were recycled into productive assets by the new owners. After identifying several potential sites in the Northeast, I contacted the owners to see if they would be interested in selling or leasing their property.

I met an elderly gentleman, Frohman Anderson, in Dighton, Massachusetts, who owned such a site and had shared my dream of converting it to an ultra-secure data depository. He did not have the financial resources to pull this off, so he was very interested in meeting a young, aspiring entrepreneur with whom he could partner. Of course at the time I didn't have the financial wherewithal to pull this off either. We hit it off well, and over the next year met numerous times and shared many a meal together discussing our shared vision. There was a large difference in our age, he was eighty-three and I was thirty-eight, but that never was an obstacle to our relationship. Frohman did not want to sell the property, so we decided we would lease it for a long-term period and accomplish our goal. I should add that this property of thirty-four acres was in very poor shape, as it had been neglected for some thirty years after the Defense Department closed the sites in the 1960s.

Frohman and I continued to discuss and negotiate. He instructed his attorney to prepare the lease. I had the lease on my desk and was in the process of reviewing and working with my attorney to complete the final deal when *the unexpected happened.*

It was a Monday morning, and my operations manager walked into my office. He said I may want to sit down, as he had some bad news to share. He proceeded to put Frohman's obituary on my desk. Frohman had dropped dead at Green Airport, in Rhode Island, over the weekend. Suddenly, the dream evaporated. Two years of work had just been wasted. A two-inch by two-inch article in the Providence newspaper had just knocked the wind out of this entrepreneur.

In respect to Frohman and his family, I dropped the project for several weeks and contemplated whether I should continue or whether this dream was gone for good with Frohman's unexpected death.

It would have been easy to give up on this project after two years of diligent effort came to a screeching halt with Mr. Anderson's death. But I refused to throw in the towel, as I was determined to complete my dream and have an underground record center.

After the hiatus it dawned on me that Frohman had three grown children, and no doubt he left the site to them. Would they want it, or, rather, would they want the money if someone was to purchase the site? I had met his attorney while negotiating the lease, so I called him to ask if he was representing the children and would they want to sell or lease the site to me. He said, "Bud, they probably would if they owned the site, but their father had willed the site to Union College in Schenectady, New York." The plot thickened.

At that, several people advised me to throw in the towel. It seemed that it just wasn't in the cards for DataVault to possess its own missile site for the storage of critical data. But I was determined.

Frohman's attorney informed me that the college had retained one of those big, fancy, and very expensive law firms to conduct the sale of the missile site, as the college wanted cash so they could form a scholarship fund.

I am not a big fan of lawyers, and the one handling this asset was an arrogant jerk. He decided that the site was worth considerably more than I had offered and that we were trying to take advantage. He would show me by reaching out to all my competitors, as he was sure they would pay much more than me. So the dance started. The attorney contacted all the players to see if they wanted to submit a bid. I prevailed, spent a little more than I wanted, but ended up owning the site rather than leasing it as we had originally planned.

This little project took nearly three years to consummate, and I still had to spend over $1,000,000 to rehab it and construct a building. My persistence was rewarded because several years later I sold the company, as well as the missile site, to Iron Mountain, a large publicly traded company.

Expect the unexpected, and you will not be disappointed. When that event does happen, walk away for a few days and do not act rashly. Regroup, rethink, and decide the best course of action. Perseverance and grit are necessary when building a company from scratch. That day will come, and you need to prepare for it.

— Chapter Thirty-One —

The Customer
Is Always Right

This is probably one you have never heard before. Yeah, right. We have heard this idiom for years. But all too often we forget it. There are two situations I want to reference: first, the new sales prospect, and, two, the existing customer who has a problem.

Sales first. We have a prospect and have been working on an opportunity for a long time. Many salespeople are far more concerned about *talking* rather than *listening*. I have seen this hundreds of times. That salesperson is fresh off of a national training session and wants to blow me away with their product knowledge. The problem is, they talk too much. They should be asking me a lot of open-ended questions, probing and looking for points of pain or hot buttons. They need to find three to five of my hot buttons and explain how their product or service will solve my problems. Instead, they focus on features of their service, whether or not those features are something that will provide benefit to me, the prospect. When they ultimately lose the sale to the competitor, they blame it on the prospect. He didn't know what he was talking about, he was just interested in the price, and he didn't like me. The list goes on and on. If you talk about you and not your prospect, your focus is in the wrong place, and you will lose the order.

It is all about the customer.

The second case is the existing customer, in which you are trying to solve a service issue. We were nonresponsive with a return call to fix the customer's problem, and she is upset it took us so long to react. The first thing we need to do is to focus on the customer and *listen*. Disarm the customer's anger by asking lots of questions. Even after she has told you about the incident, continue to ask if there is anything else you need to know. Continue to ask questions until you have exhausted all the possibilities. When you do reach that point, ask a final time if there is anything else you need to know about the problem and/ or incident.

Finally, ask the customer what their expectation is and what the customer would find acceptable. What would the customer expect your company to do in order to fix the problem and assure them that this issue would never happen again? Most customers, but not all, are reasonable people and will lay out a solution that may be tough but not impossible for you to accept.

You then have to evaluate their response and expectations and decide if you are willing to do what they want in order to preserve the relationship. Occasionally, it the customer creates expectations that are unreasonable, you may be better off to walk away and lose the account. However, in most cases, the work and costs associated with preserving the customer relationship are warranted and worthwhile.

Being in the services business for a great many years, I have faced numerous challenging or disgruntled customers. I will say that in well over 90 percent of the cases we were always able to resolve the issue to the customer's satisfaction and convince them we had taken corrective actions to assure this problem would never be repeated. When you find yourself in this situation, it is only the customer's opinion that matters relative to the resolution of the problem. You, or your people, may think you did the right thing and fixed the problem, but if the customer does not agree, you have failed.

One of our most devastating losses at AmeriVault was with an organization that dealt with workmen's compensation insurance. We had a three-year relationship with the account and had performed extremely well for that entire period. We experienced a problem, had done everything we could to restore the customer's confidence and had failed . We had lost their trust and could not regain it. Although we went to the CEO and tried to convince her that her manager was being totally unreasonable in the matter, we lost the deal.

The reason I am sharing this story with you is that it is important to define success and failure with your clients. In any business you need to define the rules of engagement with the client or prospect. In technology and service companies, these rules are referred to as SLAs or service-level agreements. They clearly spell out for the customer what service level to expect and the remedy if the vendor fails to deliver on those service levels. That remedy could be a credit or price reduction for the following month. Be sure to set clear expectations with your client, and then it will be possible to exceed those expectations on a continuous basis.

— Chapter Thirty-Two —

A Sense of Humor
Is Important

I have said it repeatedly; starting a new company is not for the faint of heart. It is hard work, with a magnitude of heavy lifting. Nothing gets you through tough times better than a good sense of humor.

One of the best places to exert your humor is through marketing themes and campaigns. I feel customers prefer to do business with fun people, people who have and show a sense of humor. You can be in a very serious business but at the same time demonstrate to your prospects and customers that you have a good sense of humor. Let me share some fun marketing campaigns that my companies have done over the past several years.

Early in my entrepreneurial career we created a fake ransom note, the kind made by cutting letters out of a magazine and pasting them into a letter, telling our customer that we were holding critical secret data tapes of their company at ransom. The letter very clearly noted that this was not real but rather a marketing campaign to point out the risk if the company did not store their vital data in a safe place—like our underground Nike missile site. Although it was very clearly noted that *this is only a marketing campaign*, some people missed that and alerted the

FBI. We got a bit embarrassed by this inquiry but clearly made our point and got some free, if not complimentary, publicity.

Then there was *Data Vault Man*. I am not sure why, but I have a thing for superheroes. DataVault Man lived in the underground missile site and was the ultimate protector of the customer's vital corporate data tapes. We had a series of comic strips drawn by a professional artist that detailed how DataVault Man was saving the world as well as saving America's corporate records from a series of villains that were trying to steal them. It was a fun and educational way to keep our name in front of the prospects and customers. And it certainly stood out from all the other marketing messages the customer received.

In the early days of AmeriVault, I bought over one thousand small prescription pill bottles, the amber-colored ones with the white top. We printed a tasteful label that said: "This is the prescription for data loss headaches. Take two of the enclosed pills and call AmeriVault for the prescription to lost and/or stolen data." The several pills we put in each bottle were sugar candy and (of course) were harmless. Unfortunately, one terribly serious prospect overreacted and wrote a nasty e-mail suggesting that we were setting a bad example by sending "drugs" through the U.S. mail. We immediately suspended the campaign. I am happy to report we had a delighted nursery school when we gave them all the plastic bottles to use for a variety of creative projects.

Finally, there was Captain Backup, a distant relative of the original DataVault Man. At AmeriVault, we started a new company, Certified Backup. This was a lower-cost backup solution for small companies. We had a great time with Captain Backup and created a lot of laughs inside the company. The highlight was when we filmed a Web video of Captain Backup with my marketing director filming Captain Backup stretched across two ladders while I sat underneath with a large fan trying to blow his cape to make him look like he was flying. We were all laughing so hard it added to the challenge of the shoot, but in the end we were successful. Captain Backup was a huge success both inside and outside the company.

Humor is a healthy tonic for the entrepreneurial company. A sense of humor contributes to the company culture and makes everyone feel good. It will certainly help get you through those trying times that are part of any entrepreneurial journey.

— CHAPTER THIRTY-THREE —

You Must Look Successful

Success breeds success. Nobody wants to take the risk of doing business with a loser. It is incredibly important to look very successful in the early days of a start-up. It gives the customer confidence that you are successful and will be around for a long time. As I have mentioned earlier, prospects will often select an adequate product or service from a very large company (IBM for example), as it reduces the risk for the decision maker. So look successful and instill confidence in your prospect's mind.

I am not suggesting you have antique tables and oriental rugs in the reception area, but look good. If you are the type of company that never has prospects visit, then this is less important. But most companies that sell goods and services to other businesses will have prospects visit for a site tour or customer visit as part of the due diligence process in making a vendor selection. A site visit can easily close the deal and eliminate the competition. It can also push the prospect towards your competitor.

What are some of the things that allow you to look successful without busting the budget?

The Web site. We talked earlier that this is the way to level the playing field. One can build and host a first-class Web site today for very modest dollars, (under $1,000). Conversely, I have seen successful companies with a terrible Web presence, and this is a big turnoff. The thought might be, if you cannot have a slick Web site you're probably a loser. Today, the Web will be the first impression you make on a visitor so don't blow it, as that visitor is probably gone for good, and you don't get a second chance. Also, when someone does visit your Web site, respond quickly and professionally. This is called lead generation; this is why you have a Web site. If someone asks for information, or a quote or a demo, *respond, and do it quickly and professionally*.

A nice office. I have advocated for getting out of the house when you launch. Commercial real estate is abundant and very affordable today, so get B-plus type space. There are some fabulous deals in real estate now, and you can get first-class space without spending much money. You can also sign a one-year lease or even month to month, which is something you cannot do when the economy is more robust. Take advantage of this market by securing some attractive office space for your employees and visitors. You don't need A space; nor do you need C-minus space. Remember, it is not just for your guests that visit; you and your staff will spend upwards of fifty hours a week there, or sometimes a lot more. Create a desirable working environment.

During the visit, have your spouse, your college daughter, or a neighbor sit out front and greet the client when they arrive and offer them coffee. I am tired of visiting an empty reception area that might have a phone so the visitor can call someone inside. At my company, one of our greatest assets was Gail, a delightful receptionist that greeted our visitors, including the UPS guy, with a large smile and a kind word. I had many positive comments from our visitors about how fabulous and fresh Gail was, and what a great first impression she made. Get yourself a Gail, even if you need to borrow her for a day; it will pay dividends.

Dress up. Yes, we are in a dress-down environment, but break the mold. My company has casual dress. It includes shorts and jeans during the summer months except for days when we have outside guests. Then everyone dresses up a bit, just business casual, and our managers wear business suits. Well-dressed managers are such an anomaly today that people will notice and remember. Our business world, in this author's opinion, has become way too casual, and that includes attitudes as well as dress. Wow, you must think I am a very old guy with old-guy ideas. I am also a guy who has built multiple successful companies.

Collateral, brochures, and handouts are less used today because of the Web and PDFs. I believe there should be at least one professional brochure. Make it expensive, high class, and memorable, and do not print it on your office printer. A couple of hundred expensive brochures will last you a long time. Ditto with business cards. They should be classy and on very good card stock. By the way, *everybody* in my former company had their own personalized business card, including Gail.

If you sell a service, and there are significant dollars attached, write the customer an impressive proposal that spells out the value you deliver and the reasons the prospect should become *your* customer. It can be a Word document that you e-mail to the client, but it can still be highly professional.

Have a great logo. And show it off on everything. Spend a few bucks to do it right, as it is your signature. You can find companies on the Internet that will design a first-class logo for you for a few hundred dollars. A logo is your corporate signature, so do it early, and do it right. You will have it for the life of the company and perhaps beyond.

Business shows in many industries are becoming passé or are being replaced by virtual shows. However, assuming you do shows and events, have a professional booth and get some high-class golf shirts to wear so everyone at the show is coordinated.

There are many ways to look successful, and you don't have to spend a lot of money to achieve it. If I visit your company on the Web or in person, and you don't make a strong first impression, I will likely move on to your competitor. Invest the time, the money, and the effort, and make a strong impression. That effort will pay dividends.

— Chapter Thirty-Four —

Beware the Union
at All Costs

Recently, we have been bombarded by continual bad news about the big three automakers and the billions we have given them and the billions more they may need. (How come I cannot get a bailout as a small businessman?) Although there are numerous reasons that General Motors and Chrysler (Ford refused the bailout) are dismal failures, there is no doubt in this writer's mind that reason number one is the union. For years management (that may be an oxymoron when talking about the big three automakers) has given the union anything they wanted. This resulted in driving wages, health care, and pension costs to the point of no return. And every so often, usually at contract time, management and the union wage war with one another, and it becomes downright nasty and hostile. What kind of company culture is that? Have they heard about working as a *team*? Are these people complete idiots? This is no way to run a business and most certainly not a successful one.

Is it any wonder that union membership that once covered nearly 40 percent of the American workforce now includes just 10 percent of a much bigger workforce? The UAW is a dinosaur, and unions do not work in most industries.

As a start-up you may not have to worry about a union organizing, but at some point you will. Do everything in your power to thwart the effort before it gets any momentum. It will destroy your company.

Business is too hard not to do it right. Camaraderie, mutual respect, team, open communication between management and everyone else in the company is absolutely mandatory if you want to succeed. Labor unions don't buy that. Rather, they foster the attitude that management is the enemy. You will have a great many challenges to overcome in the coming years. Do *not* include a union on that list!

If it sounds like I am antiunion, I have done my job.

BUD'S BOTTOM LINE TAKEAWAYS

- The glass is always half full—even when it is half empty
- Expect the unexpected
- The customer is always right—even when they are wrong
- A sense of humor will help you get through the tough times
- Look successful until you become successful

— CHAPTER THIRTY-FIVE —

YOU CAN LOOK GREAT
ON THE WEB

The Web has become one very powerful marketing tool in a very short period of time. If you are a start-up, the Web permits you to have the look and feel of a much larger, more established company than you actually may be in the early years. On the Web, a fledgling start-up can have the same look and feel as a hundred-million-dollar multinational company that has been around for decades.

Invest in the Web on day one. Better still, before you launch. It's quick and inexpensive to build and host a Web site. You *must* find a qualified Web designer and build a quality site. It can pay huge dividends. There are a great many hosting companies that will host a site for as little as $10 a month—quite a bargain. Those same companies will design and build a Web site for as low as a few hundred dollars. Using one of these companies to build your first site is fine; just get it done and up and running. You can continue to improve and grow your site as the company and your finances grow. It does not have to be perfect from Day One. I would much rather you have a Web site on opening day than not have one because you are trying to make it perfect.

Building a Website and hosting one does not necessarily mean that you will have people finding you on the Web. That does not just happen. You need to work on it to build traffic—visitors to your Web site.

Web marketing today is the most efficient and cost-effective way to market your company. If you know nothing about it, go find a good company or consultant (But don't be tricked; see my chapter on the bad consultant.) to develop a strategy for your company. Building traffic to the site is a huge new science and takes time. Once you do start generating traffic, respond quickly and professionally to Web inquiries. It is surprising how many companies spend a lot of dollars on Web marketing but fail to respond to inquiries on a timely basis.

As far as marketing and lead generation, the Web delivers more bang for the buck than any other marketing tools you might deploy. Most customers utilize the Web to research goods and services that they are planning on purchasing. Searching the Web for companies and services is the most used way to find those services. You will be judged by your Web site and how you present information. This is the first impression people will have of your business, which will have a huge impact on branding and credibility. Use it well.

One of the best ways to identify a Web prospect is to offer them something *of value* on your Web site. For example, if I was a bank offering mortgages, perhaps I could offer a mortgage calculator on my Web site or offer a white paper about the current $8,000 tax credit for first-time buyers. The trick is, you would need to provide your name, phone number, and e-mail address (maybe more data but not too much, as that turns people off) to my Web site in order to download the white paper or results of the calculator. That way you have captured the critical data about the prospect, which allows you to follow up with an e-mail or phone call. Voila, you now have a potential customer.

Of course, a great Web site is not of much value if nobody ever visits your site. You must learn about and invest in search engines and utilizing them to drive traffic to your Web site. I would urge you to invest most of your marketing budget in a variety of search engines. Go slow at first and increase your monthly budget as you become more adept at generating contacts and leads. There are hundreds of resources and Web sites and companies dedicated to search engine optimization, many of which provide excellent free content about the subject.

But do it. Utilizing search engines to generate prospects, in my view, is the optimum and most cost-effective way to generate prospects for your new business.

— Chapter Thirty-Six —

DIFFERENTIATE OR DIE

There are only four ways to differentiate your business from your competition: price, service, product, or distribution channel. And make no mistake, you must differentiate from your competition to be successful in business.

If you look exactly like all of your competitors, you are not going to survive. Why should a customer leave his established supplier to do business with the new company if you are pretty much identical? The incumbent has an advantage, and unless you give the client a reason to change, he won't.

There are only four ways to differentiate yourself from the competition, and you need to think this through, strategically, as it is important and long-lasting.

Most new companies tend to differentiate on price because they *assume* they must charge less than the competition in order to steal away business. This is the first way to differentiate and may be your choice. Do you *want* to be the low-cost provider and are you *capable* of being the low-cost provider? The danger is that no matter how low your price, there is always someone who will come along and undercut it. The low-price leader is a strategy, but your costs must match your retail price in order for this to succeed. If you are an IT services company, as we are, you cannot have high-priced, bulletproof, redundant infrastructure and manage to be the low-price provider. It just is not possible. The customer buying the low-cost or economy solution does not expect to have the very expensive infrastructure. If you chose to differentiate on price, it is essential that you have low costs, so you can still have healthy margins at your market-leading price.

Service is the next way to distinguish yourself. But you can't just say, "We have great service." Everyone says that, and good service should be a given. When we were in the traditional data storage business and delivered computer tapes using vans, the standard emergency delivery time was four hours. The market leader did that, and everyone else mimicked the industry leader. We created a new delivery standard which guaranteed a two-hour delivery. If we missed by minutes the customer did not pay. No one in New England had ever before promised a money-back guarantee; rather, they promised to try hard. We significantly raised the bar because the customer cared! There was a money-back guarantee, and over time all our competitors were forced to match our two-hour delivery guarantee. This two-hour guarantee was great for employee morale as well, as it was our holy grail. Everyone in the company knew the importance of this guarantee, and all of us, regardless of rank, would jump into our vehicle to deliver a tape and beat the guarantee whenever necessary. It built pride and great camaraderie throughout the business. This is an example of how a company can differentiate based on service.

The third way to differentiate is based on product or service. This means selling a service that is substantially different, and better, than those products already available to customers. When I launched AmeriVault over a decade ago, we pioneered a new way of doing data backup. This was a paradigm shift. The old way involved backing up to tape and having a courier in a van take the tapes to a safe building far away. Our solution used software, bandwidth, and data centers to provide a faster, better, more secure (and now) very cost-effective way to do backup. It is a far superior solution that, over time, will totally displace the old solution. It is a disruptive technology. Disruptive technology is a very good thing if you are trying to differentiate from the competition based on product or service. It might take time if you are early with a new technology, but if the service is compelling it will prevail over time. Just make sure you have the patience and capital to sustain you through that time.

The last way to differentiate is distribution. The best and most widely spread change is the Internet. There are a great many industries that have been transformed by the World Wide Web. Real estate brokers, travel, airlines, shopping, yellow pages, selling maps (why would you buy a map?), and scores of others have been materially transformed via the Internet. This is very good if you are the transformer but bad if you are an incumbent who refuses to accept the new technology.

You need at least one of these four differentiators to succeed. If you combine two or more of the four, your chances of success will be enhanced. You must give the customer a reason to move away from the incumbent and do business with you.

— CHAPTER THIRTY-SEVEN —

THE SALES GUY MYTH

I am a serial entrepreneur; I am a founder, president, CEO, boss, and many other things. But first and foremost, I am a *sales guy* and *proud of it*. I am very good at it. I consider it a most honorable profession, and it is hard to be successful. Most people on this planet could not be successful selling a product or service to a total stranger, and many would be petrified at just the thought of it.

There is a myth that the successful salesperson is slippery, fast, does magic, fools the client, is in it for themselves, is less than 100 percent honest, and is fast talking—a description we most often think of when referring to the "used car salesman." Some refer to what we do as "the game." You have heard it all before. What is your game? What game are you in? I am in the sales game, as in, to win the game one has to outsmart his or her opponent. Well, I get really ticked off when I hear someone, usually not in the game, refer to professional salespeople in such a demeaning manner. To this sales guy, there is no more demanding or challenging role within a company (including the CEO or founder) than the successful salesperson.

You need sales to survive. As I have stated repeatedly in other chapters, you need customers to survive and thrive. It is the salesperson who gets those customers to sign on the dotted line, and he or she is the lifeblood of any start-up company.

If this image of the salesperson is dead wrong, what, in fact, is the truth about the successful professional salesperson? There are numerous things, not all of which can be discussed in this chapter; but I will give you an overview of how I see things. Some of the things that the successful salesperson has or does every day are the following:

- Has very good product knowledge
- Believes 100 percent in the product or service
- Is highly organized
- Can reschedule without it becoming overwhelming
- Is great at follow-up
- Has enormous perseverance and can bounce back from repeated nos
- Is a good communicator and *a great listener*
- Understands the sales process and replicates it in every selling situation
- Doesn't get misdirected by the talkative or indifferent prospect
- Can distinguish in fifteen minutes a real prospect from a suspect
- Can negotiate and get a win/win for the company and for the customer
- Does exactly what she says she will do and never embellishes the company or the service beyond what the client can and will expect
- Sticks with a qualified prospect for sufficient time, even if it takes many months to close the order
- Has empathy for the customer and wants the customer to benefit from the sales and walks away if the value is not there for the client
- Is great at asking open-ended questions and uncovering the customer's needs and/or pain points

as well as aligning the benefits of the service to solve those needs

- Is motivated by success and, yes, by *money*
- Revels in a win. The big ones are best, but consummating the order and getting a new customer is the goal and gives the much-sought-after feeling of success

If you have ever tried to be in sales, you know of what I speak. It is hard and demanding work. It is compounded, in a start-up, by the fact you have no customers and no references, probably have an unimpressive balance sheet, have not been in business very long, and have a host of other issues as a brand new company. Being the sales guy, and you often are as the founder, in a new company with no customers and no track record is a very hard job, but a job that needs to be done.

The successful and professional salesperson will overcome all those obstacles and get those first ten clients. It will then get easier after you have those first clients as references. Either *you* have to be that salesperson, or you need to hire that salesperson. If you are not that sales guy or gal, figure it out early and go out and hire that person early. This is not an option; it is an absolute must. If you don't, the company will fail.

— Chapter Thirty-Eight —

Barter for Business

Barter, according to the World Book Dictionary, is to trade by exchanging one kind of goods or services for other goods and services without using money.

This is the section of the book where we are talking about sales and marketing, and it is longer than some other sections due to the fact that I consider it so very important to your launch. You can have the best, most technologically advanced product or service on the planet, but if you cannot convince customers to buy it, there is no business success story. Getting your product or service to customers and convincing them it solves a need for them is a key to your success.

There are traditional sales and there are nontraditional sales. I want you to be aware of and consider as many successful sales strategies as possible to enhance your chance for success. Barter is another strategy.

Barter goes back to caveman days. Early settlers and American Indians used barter all the time (there were no Visa cards). Barter is a custom and practice that literally has been around since the beginning of time.

- I have bartered office equipment for furniture.
- I have traded microfilming services for an inground swimming pool.

- I have traded data storage for catering services.
- I have bartered online backup for earth shoes; all of my twenty-four employees got two pairs each.
- And I have traded IT services with NFL teams for marketing and advertising.

There were some other less noteworthy bartering experiences in my career, and I am just one small businessman that did all this. Imagine the possibilities.

You must do all of this while observing tax rules and regulations, which I always did. I am not advocating doing this surreptitiously to avoid paying taxes. You need to declare and pay taxes where *applicable*, but it is a viable sales strategy.

You may have a prospect or customer who would like to procure your service but does not currently have budget monies available to make the purchase. This is a perfect situation where barter may work for you. Just ask the question: Does your company ever barter for goods and services? Many companies do.

You may choose to do a partial barter or trade and also use part cash. The example I gave of trading backup for shoes was actually half cash and half barter. The customer really had a need for our backup services and was more than willing to pay for our services but did not have sufficient budget. Doing a transaction with both cash and barter was a win/win for both companies.

There are also a great many barter groups today. Barter groups or trade exchanges are networks of hundreds of companies that belong to the exchange. If I sell my service to another member for $2,000, I then get a $2,000 credit that I may use at any of the member companies. The beauty of this concept is that there is a vast array of services to trade. Therefore, if I do not have a need for my client's product, I can pick from other merchants' products or services that I do need.

Barter is a great concept. It expands your ability to get customers. Right now we are in a challenging economic time,

Bud Stoddard

and you need to be as creative as possible to win sales and win customers. Barter may be a tool that will allow you to capture a customer that you may not have won without the barter component. There are a great many things you need when you start your business, and barter may get you some while conserving your cash.

— Chapter Thirty-Nine —

Sales ... Warm Call ... Don't Cold Call

In my view, being able to sell is the most critical success factor in establishing (business to business) a company. You must generate sales, and to do that, you need customers. In my last company we sold IT services, specifically online backup and disaster recovery and related services. Our prospect is the IT director, CIO (Chief Information officer) or the CFO (chief financial officer) of small to midsize companies in all industries. (I define that as forty to four hundred employees.)

The challenge is that hundreds, perhaps thousands, of salespeople are targeting the CIO of a midsized law firm or investment company. That CIO is likely getting ten to forty cold calls per day from someone who wants to sell their product or service. That sales rep thinks his or her product, and rightfully so, is the greatest thing since sliced bread, and the prospect cannot live without it. Cold calling that prospect is a total waste of time. The likelihood of you reaching that person on the phone and securing an appointment to pitch your product is less that 1 percent. Yet thousands of companies continue to have their sales reps cold call these prospects and wonder why they get disappointing results.

Additionally, relative to gaining new prospects, the yellow pages are a dinosaur and trade shows are very expensive. You can easily spend 10k to 15k on a major trade show in a major city. You'll be hard pressed to meet any *real* prospects. About the only thing that will get accomplished is giving away hundreds of pens or key chains with your logo on them. Forget it. There is no return on investment with this practice.

Two years ago, we stopped participating in all trade shows. At the time we were spending $150,000 per annum on ten to fifteen trade shows in different parts of the country. We took that money and got serious about search. (Google, Yahoo, Microsoft, Ask, etc.) In short, we bought a lot of keywords that described the services we sell so that if a prospect googled "online backup," "offsite storage" or "internet backup," they had a reasonably good chance of finding AmeriVault on page one of the search results.

"Search" is a very complex subject today, and it is not as easy as throwing a stack of money to Google. We took several months and really learned a lot about the search business. There are hundreds of resources and consultants that you can utilize to learn how to deploy the Web and the many search engines for the purpose of lead generation. There are also many "alleged experts" who would lead you to believe that they know about search. Be cautious and do a complete due diligence on any consultant before you hire them, and verify that they really are subject experts.

Getting the most out of the Web is not just about buying keywords; it is also about *natural search*. Your placement on search, page one versus page eleven, is about *natural search*. In short, this is determined by where and how often your company is mentioned on the Web, on other search engines, on blogs, in press releases, in subject articles, and the like. The more exposure you get, the greater impact that will have on your ranking relative to natural search. Substantially improving your ranking is something that will require a strategy, expertise, and a budget, but the results are well worth it.

Following is the most important point of this chapter, the one thing I want you to take away.

The likelihood of cold calling a C-level executive prospect the very day that he or she is thinking about your particular service and having a need for that service, (oh, and budget too) and engaging them live by phone for ten minutes to discuss that need is *zero*.

Yet historically, virtually all business to business companies have conducted sales and new customer acquisition in this manner. (And I admit I have done the exact same thing over and over in starting five companies.) Salespeople make hundreds of cold calls to C-level executives at target companies with the hope of reaching them by phone and having a conversation about their product or service. This is a wasteful activity and frustrating to your salespeople as well. I recently spoke with one of my CIO customers, who told me he gets forty cold calls per day from salespeople and doesn't listen to *any of them*. In fact, he has a separate voice mail box to receive all of these calls, which his assistant empties at the end of each day.

Do not do it. You will waste hundreds of hours, become extraordinarily frustrated, and get no results from this action.

The Web has changed life and business forever. When the prospect is about to purchase products or services for her company, it is highly likely that she will utilize search engines to do research and find suppliers to interview. Work smarter, not harder, and think outside the box. Getting customers, as I have said repeatedly, is absolutely necessary to building a successful company. You need to figure out a time-effective and cost-effective way to accomplish that in your company.

Although there are many good ideas in this little book, this is a critical one that all by itself will pay for the price of the book (unless you got it for free) a hundred times over.

Don't forget it; write it down; it is money. I absolutely guarantee it.

— Chapter Forty —

Sales ... Remove the Risk

You are in a real sales situation. The prospective decision maker has demonstrated some interest in your product or service. He has a need, the budget is not an issue, and he has the ability to pay. You are a new company (less than ninety days old), have a couple of employees, little or no revenue, no financial staying power, no references or track record. And you expect the prospect to just say *yes*?

Unfortunately, it is probably not going to happen. You have enormous energy and have presented your service with the facts and demonstrated your passion. The prospect has pain (more on pain later), and you both agree that your product or service will eliminate his pain or problem.

But you have no customers and nobody wants to be first. *Remove the risk.*

Every new company has been in exactly this position on many occasions in their young careers. And more often than not, they walk away without securing the business but do not know why.

Most of the time a prospect does not make a decision because he or she fears it will be a bad one. We have all heard about FUD—fear, uncertainty, and doubt. Many large companies have been successful in selling adequate, overpriced products or services when the smaller, more innovative competitor had a better, more cost-effective, higher-quality solution. But the larger company convinced the prospect that nobody ever got fired for choosing them. This happens hundreds of times every day. The prospect buys the lesser-quality solution from the big, well-known, financially successful supplier because he or she doesn't perceive any risk in that decision. The decision is made based on minimizing risk.

Thus, remove the risk in order to improve your chances of success. Persuade the customer your service is better than the competition. Convince the customer that you will give them an unbelievable price, better than any other. I once traded shoes for my service in order to get our price down because the prospect had little money and lots of shoes. Convince the customer that he will get incredible service twenty-four hours a day, seven days a week, 365 days per year.

Then take the risk out. Give the customer a guaranteed sixty-day no-risk guarantee that sounds something like this: If for any reason we do not exceed (not meet) your expectations during the first sixty days, we will give you a full refund, shake hands, and walk away. We want *you* to be the sole judge (not us) of whether we exceed your expectations.

Trust me, this works! You must give it a try.

— Chapter Forty-One —

BE OPPORTUNISTIC IN YOUR SALES PROCESS

I have founded five companies over the past twenty-five years, all having to do with the information capture, data protection, and storage business. At my first company, Micromedia, we filmed millions of documents for companies, capturing the images on roll microfilm or microfiche. We primarily utilized products and supplies, including film, from the Eastman Kodak Company. Back in the 1980s Kodak was by far the industry leader in the micrographics industry. During that time we formed numerous relationships with Kodak salespeople with the hopes they would introduce us to their customers and prospects.

Kodak had a new and expensive technology called Oracle that embossed a unique bar code on each film image and had proprietary film readers that found the image based on the bar code. This was industry-leading technology that allowed the user to find one of thousands of images in seconds, where previously this manual search would take much longer.

Digital Equipment Corporation was a prominent computer manufacturer in the Northeast and was one of the largest employers in Massachusetts. DEC, as they were known, was later acquired by Compaq and later by Hewlett Packard. DEC was a large Kodak customer and was anxious to deploy the new Oracle coding technology and was planning to acquire the Oracle cameras, which at the time cost in excess of $30,000 each. This would have been one of the first purchases of the new technology in the Northeast and was a marquee customer for Kodak. The Kodak salesperson had worked on the order for months and was very excited about getting this major win. Everything was moving forward in the right direction.

Suddenly, the wheels fell off, bringing the sale to a grinding halt, when Digital announced a freeze on all new capital expenditures. The minicomputer business was at risk due to the advent of the IBM PC, and DEC was desperate to slash expenses, in particular capital expenditures.

In a meeting with my Kodak rep, not the DEC salesperson, I suggested that my company would step up and purchase the camera if Digital, in turn, would sign a two-year agreement to buy imaging services from Micromedia. This would then guarantee me an income stream over a multiyear period. Kodak would still get the sale; Digital would reap the benefit of getting all their documents filmed with the new Kodak technology, and Micromedia would get a significant new piece of business with a major account. We would also become an industry expert with Kodak's newest technology. This was *win/win/win*—a win for Digital, a win for Kodak, and certainly a win for my small company, MicroMedia.

We successfully negotiated the contract with DEC and wrote a purchase order for the Kodak Oracle camera. We were a very young company at the time and undercapitalized. This was a major step in our ultimate success. Because we thought outside the box and took advantage of a unique opportunity, we secured a large repeat customer who normally would have not been a client.

This is a classic example of what I mean by *opportunistic sales.*

Fast forward several years to 2004. I had been trying for many months to secure the business of the world champion

New England Patriots for my fourth company, AmeriVault, now called Venyu. AmeriVault is a leader in the online data backup and disaster recovery business. I knew their team had a significant need for our services, as the organization is highly data dependant and, at the time, had a less than proficient solution for data protection.

I had unsuccessfully tried to secure an appointment with their CIO for nearly one year. Finally, after numerous attempts, she agreed to give me an introductory meeting. Timing was finally good, and she was interested in hearing our story and learning how AmeriVault might help her do a better job at data backup and recovery. After a couple of additional meetings and a proposal, the opportunity was there to secure them as an account. Unfortunately, they were doing business with a competitor. It was a much larger firm than us. They were a corporate sponsor of the New England Patriots and spent a lot of money for sponsorship activities. The CIO liked what we had to offer but told me they preferred to do business with companies that were corporate sponsors of the team. As we had a limited marketing budget, we really didn't have the kind of funds (over 65k per year) necessary to become a team sponsor.

I saw another opportunity to think outside the box to secure the client. I suggested to the CIO that perhaps we could barter backup services for marketing assets with the team. We would become their backup vendor and bill them for our services. However, we would also purchase marketing services and reduce our bill by the amount of the marketing spent with the team. Again, both parties win, and five years later we continue to be the official data protection company of the New England Patriots (see www.Patriots.com).

This program proved to be so successful that AmeriVault has subsequently done similar partnerships with five other NFL teams: the Baltimore Ravens, New York Jets, Atlanta Falcons, Green Bay Packers, and San Diego Chargers.

The sales process is certainly one of the most important ingredients of a successful growth company. To excel and continuously beat the competition, especially when those companies are bigger and more established, you *must* think creatively and seize opportunities that others don't see or bother to execute. Be different. Be fresh.

Be creative. Be opportunistic! You will win business that others don't see.

— Chapter Forty-Two —

Sales People Need to Be Paid Commissions

How should I pay my salespeople is a common question that I get from new and old entrepreneurs alike. It is very common and very important.

Salespeople are "coin operated," as it has been said. They respond to commissions, and a rich commission program will ensure you attract and keep the highest caliber of salespeople.

I have heard the argument, "I prefer to pay my people on a straight salary, with perhaps an annual bonus, as it fosters teamwork and doesn't have my salespeople competing against one another." I say "bull" to that argument. I would challenge anyone to show me a successful and effective sales force that is compensated on salary and not commission.

Salespeople are a special breed. They are highly competitive, they love to win and hate to lose, and they want to be compensated accordingly. I would recommend, at the very least, that 40 percent of the salesperson's annual compensation be variable or commission and the balance be their base salary. So, if you want your reps to make 100k per annum, I would pay them a base salary of 60k. This is a guideline only and will vary from industry to industry, but it is still a good guideline. Dependent upon price of the product or service and the annual quota, one company may pay a commission of 3 to 4 percent (1,000,000 annual quota) while another may pay commissions of 10 to 12 percent ($400,000 annual quota) to reach the same goal of $40,000 in annual commissions.

I have suggested over and over that recruiting a top-notch salesperson is absolutely critical to the success of your company. You need customers and clients, and it is the salesperson's job to find and secure those clients. And if you want to recruit and motivate that exceptional salesperson, you need to have a generous commission program that rewards *success*.

Another concept in sales is that of hunters and farmers. Hunters are those salespeople we just described, who get new business from new customers. Farmers, on the other hand, are account managers that take care of the customers once you get them. They are equally important, but they perform two different functions and should be compensated differently. Young companies generally only need hunters, the salespeople. In the early stages of a company's development, the salesperson gets the client, services the client, and continues to be paid commissions for the revenue that the client generates. At some point each salesperson will have so many clients that it becomes difficult to service the existing ones while continuing to secure new customers for the firm. At that point, I would suggest that existing clients be turned over to an account manager, or farmer, to better serve the clients, while the salesperson, or hunter, focuses on new business. Generally speaking, I would pay the account manager more salary and less commission—perhaps 80/20 versus the salesperson at 60/40. Developing a two tier sales force with hunters and farmers is probably something you don't have to worry about until the company has over 250 customers.

For starters, go get that top-notch salesperson and pay her well. Don't be afraid that your salesperson will make too much money. I hear that all the time from new entrepreneurs. "What happens if the sales rep makes too much money?" *Fabulous.* That would mean your salesperson has exceeded expectations and brought in lots of new customers. I cannot think of a better problem I would rather have. Should this happen, you can always fix it later.

My last point on commissions is, pay them quickly and regularly. The rep should be paid when the invoice is rendered to the client, *not when the customer pays the invoice*. Pay commissions regularly and on a schedule—twice per month or once per month on the fifteenth for all sales that billed during the previous month. Don't make the salespeople wait to get paid. They work hard to win the business, so you need to work hard to pay commissions on a timely basis.

If you have a company that depends on outside salespeople for your success, highlight this chapter and refer to it regularly, as there is good stuff here.

— Chapter Forty-Three —

Sales: Know Your Product Well and Know Theirs Better

I am a lifelong salesperson, and I love the art of sales. I enjoy meeting with salespeople and critiquing their effectiveness. I go into a sales interview (as a prospect) with expectations based on the company that the salesperson represents. I assume if the rep works for a large company with an excellent sales reputation, that they have had hundreds of hours of training and product knowledge and will be very good at their craft.

I have two pet peeves in sales interviews. One is when the sales rep talks 90 percent of the time and leaves thirty minutes later (the degree of my patience) knowing nothing about me, my company, or my needs. (See my chapter on listening.) The second frustration is when I question the rep about their major competitors, and they don't know the competition. They usually revert to telling you how they are the best but cannot tell you why or point out differences to the competitor because they do not *know* the competitor's strengths and weaknesses.

A favorite company of mine, and one I respect greatly, is EMC. Several years ago, EMC was guilty of the behavior I just described. They were on top of the world, highly arrogant, hired lots of former jocks, and had freshly financed dot-com companies waiting in line to buy terabytes of storage from their company. At the time we were an EMC customer and were ready to make our biggest buy ever and become an exclusive EMC shop if we got what we wanted. Our company was small but was growing very well in the data backup business. We were making storage purchases three to four times per annum and so were a sought-after client by many companies in that business. We had the big meeting, the third one with the sales rep and regional VP of sales, and we were absolutely inclined to give them the business. The sales rep, who is now in another industry, could not answer the most simple of questions. For our needs, why is EMC the right choice, and what differentiates you from companies A and B, your two major competitors? The salesperson, and others, were stumped. They could not give intelligent answers to those very simple questions. We went with the competition.

In fairness to EMC, things changed dramatically after the dot-com crash, and they have a much smarter, more humble, and harder-working sales force today. As I have enormous respect for the company and have friends there, I do not want to paint all EMC salespeople with a broad brush. Maybe I just had a bad sales guy.

It was a happy ending for them. We continued to buy a lot more Clarion storage from EMC, and to this day the company is still a large and satisfied customer of EMC.

If you expect to be successful in sales, you must know your major competitors and be able to differentiate your product or service from theirs in order to be successful. Always know your top three or four competitors and their strengths and weaknesses. If you don't know who they are, your VP of sales or CEO will know who they are. Someone at your company needs to track and monitor the top competitors and why they are winning or losing. When you lose a deal to one of those companies, and you will, know exactly why you lost.

One last thought. Pointing out the differences is not bashing the competitor. I have never allowed our sales team to bash the competitor. You can compete while taking the high road. This approach will gain the customer's respect and confidence.

— Chapter Forty-Four —

Sales Is About
Effective Listening

I have agreed to appointments with hundreds of salespeople for two reasons. One, I am always interested in observing salespeople's techniques, and, two, I may find someone really good that I would like to hire. But regardless of my motivation in agreeing to these sales appointments, there is one very important lesson that I have learned from observing salespeople. Almost without exception, salespeople talk too much and listen too little.

I am particularly surprised and disappointed when I meet with someone from a large, well-known company that has put their people through countless sales training and presentations and coaching. Often, these salespeople are so anxious to *tell me what they do* and how good they are at doing it, that they leave my office forty-five minutes later knowing little or nothing about me (the CEO), my company, or my needs. They have a one on one with the CEO (the decision maker) and have totally blown a great opportunity. They never bothered to utilize that time to determine my needs, ask lots of questions, and/or explain how their product or service will fulfill my needs. They leave the office feeling great, probably will tell their sales manager what a great call they had with my company, how well the meeting went, yet will have no clue that they have no chance to earn my business

This may be sales 101, but few people get it, and it really is pretty simple and worth remembering. A good sales call involves asking lots of open-ended questions. You need to learn about the prospect, his or her company, and their needs, why they agreed to meet with you, and what problem they are anxious to solve. This needs to be done before you recite word one of your presentation or tell them about your product or service. Samples of some effective open-ended questions or statements are the following:

- Tell me about your company, needs, problems, procedures, etc.
- How do you go about doing such and such?
- What exactly do you mean by that?
- Could you explain that issue in a little more detail?
- What will happen if you do not solve that problem?
- How long has that been an issue for you?
- Do you have a preference for outsourcing, and how do you decide to outsource versus do that internally?
- Tell me about your budgeting process.
- Have you dedicated budget funds for this project?
- What are your top three or four selection criteria for selecting a supplier?
- Are there others involved in the decision process?
- Is this a decision you want to implement in the next sixty days?

Bottom line, questions that start with how, what, where, and when are good ones. Questions that can be answered with a yes or no or a one-word answer are not.

Take notes; write everything down that you learn. It is flattering to a prospect when what he or she says is important enough for you to write it down. Write it down even if the prospect is a big bore.

Once you have asked lots of questions and even more follow-up questions, you now may begin your presentation.

As you do that, make sure you relate your features and benefits back to what the prospect talked about during the exhaustive Q&A that you just went through. Make the presentation interactive and include the prospect or prospects in the conversation—this is a conversation not a monologue. When you make a point about reliability and accuracy, for example, stop and ask the prospect if enhanced reliability is something that would improve their operation. As you complete your presentation be sure to summarize his needs (four or five things is a good number) and precisely how your service fulfills those needs. Then, seek agreement from the customer that they agree with the points you have made and agree with the statements you have made.

Sometimes, you get a nontalkative prospect, and no matter how hard you try you cannot extract a lot of information. There are certain things that most customers will agree to, and you can always fall back on these if you are in need. These would include such things as: highly automated, error free, precise, lower your costs with technology, and reduce errors, money-back guarantee, 24/7 service, very high quality, world-class reputation, reliability, guaranteed results. I can always get the nontalkative prospect to agree that four or five of these things are important to him and his company. So can you, and if you cannot, pack your bags and go on to the next prospect.

I am passionate about this subject, and most of the salespeople don't do a good job at it. Force yourself to ask lots of open-ended questions, listen to the answers, write them down, and relate your product or service to the customer's needs, and you will be well on your way to making the sale. Sounds easy, and it will be if you just follow this prescription.

And finally, listen twice as much, at least, as you talk.

— CHAPTER FORTY-FIVE —

NO PAIN EQUALS NO SALE

Earlier I talked about asking lots of good open-ended questions and determining the customer's needs. Pain is associated with the need. Does the client, or prospect, have pain from his need? Is he or she willing to spend some money to satisfy that need and remove the pain? If we have physical pain, often we take a pain reliever to make the pain go away. Your product or service needs to be that pain reliever to fulfill the need and remove the prospect's pain.

Often the salesperson will misdiagnose the problem. They do not get the sale and tell their supervisor that the prospect was cheap, had no budget, or felt our price was too high. If that happens to you, and it will, what it really means is that you did not do a good enough job *proving* to the client that your service would solve his problem and remove his pain, and the price was well worth it to accomplish that.

But first, you need to determine if the client has pain, and if the individual is committed to solving or removing that pain. Sometimes there are clearly issues, and the company has a problem it should solve, but the individual manager is not committed to fixing the problem. If there is no pain, there is no sale, regardless of the price. Let me take a real-life case study to try and bring this point home.

Our company was meeting with a very large insurance agency. The IT director agreed that their data backup was not great and that the backup data was stored in the same building, which is not safe if there is a fire or flood in the offices. After several meetings, he liked what our service did but felt we were very expensive and felt he could do it in-house exactly as *our* solution promised.

He clearly had a need, and the CFO agreed, but they both felt that our price was too high. The good news for us was that the prospect had *pain*. They had lost data, were growing quickly, and were convinced they would lose mission-critical data in the future if they did not make some changes. Additionally, they had no backup servers (computers) or a disaster recovery plan in the event they were hit by a local or regional disaster (fire, flood, hurricane, human error, disgruntled employee, collapsed roof, etc.).

Our job became to prove to the two decision makers that, one, our price was competitive with theirs and they had underestimated the *true cost* of trying to do this internally; two, our solution was far superior to the alternative, and they needed the better, more comprehensive solution; and, three, we guaranteed success, something they could not get internally. (When I say "guarantee success, " I mean, if we don't exceed your expectations, you don't pay.)

After several months and several meetings, we won the business by proving to the prospect we were cost effective, a better solution, and the results were guaranteed. The client signed a multiyear contract that exceeded $250,000.

Look for the pain rather than reducing your price. If the client has pain and the money to remove it, he is a viable prospect that can be closed. If he doesn't have pain or doesn't acknowledge it, you will never close the deal. It is that simple. Lowering the price is absolutely a worthless strategy if the prospect has no need.

Remember: No pain, no sale

BUD'S BOTTOM LINE TAKEAWAYS

- Differentiate or *die*
- *Utilize the Web to look larger and more successful than you are*
- Selling is the most important process
- Warm call, don't cold call
- Remove the risk for the customer
- Be opportunistic
- Pay your salespeople fat commissions
- Listen, listen, then listen some more
- Find the pain or leave

— Chapter Forty-Six —

Graduation Time

You are ready. Or are you?

Well, I have told you absolutely, positively everything you will ever have to know about starting your first business (or second or third). Actually, that is not true, as nobody could ever know everything. But I do think there are a lot of good ideas and thought and recommendations in this small book that could very well be the difference between success and failure.

So, are you ready or not? Tough question, isn't it? Maybe you read this book and thought you knew a lot of the things I wrote about. Maybe you felt that a *lot of this is common sense*. That would be correct. Perhaps, you felt I am not the brightest bulb in the box, and if I could start five successful companies (so far) you could certainly do much better than me.

Let me see if I can review the highlights and bring it all together for you. Section one is about preparation and taking inventory. Your main takeaways should be:

1. Want it badly.

2. Have a great attitude.

3. Write a business plan and execute.

4. Get out of the house.

5. Be sure to get complete buy-in from the spouse.

Section two is all about money and where to get it. You need some cash to launch. And remember these key thoughts:

1. Calculate your break even and double it.

2. Find an angel or friend (not your father-in-law) to invest.

3. Avoid VCs if you can.

4. Manage cash, as it is your most precious asset.

Section three is all about the people you hire. There will be issues along the way, and smart, highly committed staff will make an enormous difference. So, remember to:

1. Hire the very best people you can.

2. Make them owners in the company just like you.

3. Tell them absolutely everything, including the financial stuff.

4. Incent everyone, not just the salespeople.

Section four's takeaways include:

1. The glass is always half full.

2. The customer is always right, even when they are wrong.

3. A good sense of humor is important.

4. Look successful in the early years.

Section five is all about sales. If there is an area of expertise that is most often overlooked by new entrepreneurs, it is sales. Every new company start-up must have a sales champion. If that is you, the CEO, fine, go for it. If you are a tech or operations star but not that good in a sales role, then you absolutely must make your first or second hire the salesperson. I just cannot stress this subject enough, and a great many entrepreneurs fail right here. Think about it carefully and evaluate yourself in this role. Would you hire you as the one salesperson in the company that all success depended upon?

Our takeaways for this section are as follows:

1. Differentiate to succeed; you cannot be just like all the rest.

2. Sell, sell, sell … and then sell some more.

3. Generate leads with the Internet.

4. Listen intently and remove the risk and be opportunistic.

5. Pay fat commissions.

6. Find the pain or go away, because you are wasting your time if the customer has no pain.

It is time. The rest is up to you, as I cannot make the decision for you. In this entrepreneur's mind, doing it is a thrill like no other. It is hard; it is challenging. Most people will never do it, but if you are one of those that does, the ride will be well worth it.

Good luck.

— EPILOGUE —

I really thought I was done, retired, moving to Florida, playing golf and going to Perkins for the early bird special. I was wrong.

Shortly after departing my former company, AmeriVault, in the spring of 2009 I got a little bored. I hit 10,000 golf balls and tried my hand at early retirement but honestly I wasn't very good at it. I called Kevin Harris, my AmeriVault cofounder, and we met several times over the next few months brainstorming our next new company. Kevin was intent on starting a security company but I told him we still had things to accomplish together in data storage. When I assured him he could be the CEO this time and I would play second banana, that was all it took to convince him we needed to do this.

By the time "Reflections of a Serial Entrepreneur" is published, our new company, NextVault, will be up and running.(see what we are up to at www.nextvault.com)   Since Kevin got a pre-release copy of this book, I am highly confident that he will be a successful entrepreneur and company leader.

I guess I just wasn't ready to retire.

Bud Stoddard